Job Search Marketing

Finding Job Opportunities In Any Economy

David E. Dirks

Published by JobSearchMarketing.Net

For discounted quantity orders for this book, contact the author at:
dirksmarketing@gmail.com

ISBN: 1-4392-4902-4
ISBN-13: 9781439249024

To order additional copies, please contact us.
BookSurge
www.booksurge.com
1-866-308-6235
orders@booksurge.com

Table of Contents

Acknowledgments

When I decided to embark on this book, I had no idea where this adventure would take me or how challenging it would really be. In the course of writing this book, I have had the opportunity to take the collective ideas, insights, and experiences that have accumulated over time and turn them into something that can hopefully make a positive difference in people's lives. That is no easy task when you are staring at a blank page and trying to type your thoughts into understandable and concise sentences. That said, it is a challenge that I personally find both invigorating and professionally challenging at the same time. This book is truly a labor of love and passion.

I will also tell you that no book is ever written in a complete vacuum. The ideas and insights provided in this book come from the collective experience I have been fortunate to have in my professional and personal life so far. They are the product of the constant sharing of ideas that goes on within my network of friends and business contacts.

While I cannot thank the thousands of people who have helped me in one way or another accumulate the experiences, knowledge, ideas, and insights needed to write a book of this kind, there are a few I would like to point out and thank along the way.

Rick Bronder has been my mentor and friend for over thirty-three years, and his impact on my life has been tremendous. In ways both seen and unseen, Rick has been a central player for instilling in me the mindset that you can achieve anything you put your passion and mind to. For that insight alone, I am forever grateful to Rick.

The cover design for this book was the result of superb creative design work from my agency of choice, Focus Media (www.advertisingandpr.com). When I met with Josh Sommers, the CEO of Focus Media months before this book was completed, he eagerly took on the challenge developing a world-class cover. If you know the publishing industry, aside from having great content, a book must also have a great cover.

Josh put a design team together that consisted of Tony Morino, Marketing Director, and Chrissy Lawrence, Focus Media's Art Director. Josh, Tony, and Chrissy combined their expertise to create a cutting-edge book cover design. I cannot thank them enough for what they have done to help make this book possible.

Katie Benoit was my editor for this book, and her editorial and copywriting expertise helped to make this book a far superior product than what I produced alone in the first draft. When Katie indicated that she was interested in providing an editorial review for this book, it was a no-brainer decision for me to bring her on board for this project. Katie is an outstanding editor and has worked to make this book a better product for you, the reader.

There were many who provided additional input and insights, and they made themselves available for interviews and discussions along the way while developing this book. Thanks to Rick Bronder, Major Willie Biggin, David Meerman Scott, Steven Van Yoder, Rich Rochon, Mike Spencer, Gene Ladd, John D'Ambrosio, Dan O'Brien, Tom Dimmick, Phil Collins, Catherine Kaputa, Dan Schwabel, Jon Gordon, Andy J. Kovitz, and Paul Krupin.

Also a big thanks goes to the social networks of Ning and Facebook for helping to provide their own insights on how to leverage their social networks.

My wife, Christine, gets the most thanks for cutting me a wide girth of time and patience while I spent many hours on weekends and nights writing this book. After twenty-two years of marriage, she still gives me the benefit of the doubt when I undertake a new "project." That is the kind of love and support you cannot put a price tag on.

David E. Dirks
July 2009

Chapter 1
About This Book

This is a book about personal marketing in the context of a conducting a job search. It is a book about conducting a job search with the eyes and mindset of a marketer. It has a single-minded purpose: *to show you how to develop a job search marketing campaign that will help you uncover and build a pipeline of job leads and opportunities.*

Whatever the economic and job market conditions, *the surest way to uncover job opportunities is to be the best job seeker there is*. You'll have a very distinct advantage over your competition if you commit yourself to learning everything you can about job search strategies & tactics. Your first step was to buy this book. That was the easy part. Your next challenge is to absorb this material and internalize it so that you understand it and apply it effectively to your search campaign. The last challenge you'll have is staying the course and seeing the mission through until you are successfully employed. Staying focused and on course is where the rubber meets the road during a job search.

Throughout the course of your job search campaign, you should think of yourself as a sales and marketing expert looking to sell and promote one product: *you*. Sales and marketing experts spend their careers looking to build a pipeline of potential customers to sell products and services. They know that only a certain percentage of those potential customers will turn into real, paying customers.

Say, for example, they have ten potential customers in their sales pipeline. How many of them will convert into real customers? All ten? Probably not, and, typically, most businesses only convert a percentage of all the sales opportunities they get in front of. The same applies to the process of job search. Only a small percentage of job opportunities you find will convert into real job offers.

Therein lies the secret to your future job search success: Finding enough of the right job opportunities to allow you to convert some of them into real job offers. Like top-performing marketing and sales professionals, your mission is to create a job search marketing campaign that allows you to find a steady flow of job opportunities for your consideration. This is where I find most people have the toughest time. You cannot count on obtaining another job if your pipeline of opportunities is thin. You want to stack the odds in your favor by marketing yourself to create a constant flow of new job opportunities to consider.

Successful job search in a highly competitive world requires you to have much more than a cover letter and a résumé at the ready. You need to become a skillful marketer of your experiences, knowledge, insights, and performance history. Modern job search encompasses using many of the same cutting edge marketing strategies and tactics that are used today by high-performing, market-focused companies.

The idea of building a pipeline of job opportunities is really the key here. What business would bet their whole future on just one sales lead? Instead, top-performing businesses make it their business to market and position themselves in such a way as to create a steady flow of sales leads. This book is designed to do the same thing, only in a job search framework. Would you bank your life on only one job opportunity? It's not likely and rightly so. Being able to discover the right job opportunities and keep them flowing into your job search pipeline is where this book is vested.

Job Search Resources

Today there are more resources than ever that can be tapped to help you uncover opportunities that few are willing to invest the time and effort necessary to find. Some job searching resources just seem to get better over time with the development of new technology.

Take a resource like business networking, for instance. Good old-fashioned, face-to-face business networking has been around for a long time and is a sure-fire way to meet with and develop relationships with people who could provide you with information, contacts, or actual job opportunities. Online social networking resources such as LinkedIn and Facebook are just a few examples of additional job search tools that allow you to expand from traditional, face-to-face networking to a broader more geographically-diverse area of networking in the electronic age.

The combination of both traditional networking and social networking are powerful tools for the modern job seeker. These tools are unmatched in any time in our history in terms of allowing you to reaching out to more people in a shorter period of time than ever thought possible. Business networking is a job search marketing opportunity for you and just one of many personal marketing opportunities we will cover in this book.

Job Search Networking: A Personal Story

My first job out of college was the result of a network connection I made back when I was in the ninth grade. It was during that year of junior high school that I took my first business class. It was taught by a dynamic and well-respected teacher named Jack Roche. Attending Jack's general business class gave me my first taste of the business world, and I could not get enough of it.

I went on my way and finished high school and during that time, Jack left teaching to work as an executive on Wall Street. Having made a great and lasting impression on me, I tracked Jack down at his new digs in New York City and kept in touch. Over the years of high school and then college, I made a few trips down to Wall Street to visit Jack and get the tour of that side of the business world.

Little did I know then, nearly thirty years ago, that I was officially "networking" in the best tradition. Jack told me years later that I was the only student who made it a point to stay in contact. It was a lesson I would not forget. Just before I graduated college, Jack called me up one day. He asked me what my plans were for after graduation, and I gave him the summary. I was knee-deep in interviewing with different companies but had not finalized anything. Jack had a different plan. He had a job opportunity in his department that would take me from rural upstate New York to living and working in the heart of Manhattan.

And so, I launched my first career (human resources management) on the basis of a friendship that I had taken the time to invest in. It was a great lesson for me in the power of business networking and developing friendships. It was just the beginning of my walk through the process of learning to establish business relationships of lasting value and impact.

Every position I have held since then was the result of researching and investing time and energy into establishing a network of business relationships. As my marketing career has progressed, the network of people I know has not grown in numbers dramatically as much as it has grown in quality.

Getting to There from Here

If you have an idea of what career track you would like to be on in this stage of your life, this book is for you. If you want to learn the strategies and tactics of marketing yourself, then you have picked up the right book.

It is said that most people will end up having several careers during their lifetime and I am fortunate that I have had little trouble finding my own way. Over the past thirty years, I have had successful careers in human resources, marketing, sales, the military (via the USMC), as an outdoor columnist/writer, and a business columnist/book author. These are not just jobs I have held over the years but meaningful amounts of my life have been devoted to each of these areas (some of which I have held simultaneously). Each time I made a career transition, it required me to market and position myself favorably in the job market. It also meant that I would have to proactively market myself so that I could uncover the right job opportunities I needed at that time in my life.

I learned how to successfully overcome job search challenges by applying many of the basic marketing principals used during the course of my professional marketing career to my job search. These are presented to you in this book.

I was already learning about the power of personal branding back in the mid-80s, well before it was a hip and popular term. The concept of personal branding is not really new. People of great reputation in all fields of business have long known that reputation is everything. Now, this "reputation" is called your personal brand. Over the years, structure, process, and context have been added to the ways you can enhance your personal brand.

The tools available to you today to enhance and expand your personal brands are immensely powerful and readily available. Over the years, I have deployed both traditional and nontraditional (i.e., Web 2.0, which is fast becoming the standard for job search marketing) job search strategies and tactics. In the process, I have made mistakes and have learned from them, even when it was difficult to for me to personally acknowledge those mistakes.

This book is a strong, healthy marriage between the marketing strategies used successfully in business, business networking, and traditional job search methods. The job search marketing principles in this book are not theories; rather, they are based on a strong foundation of finding and generating job opportunities that few are willing to invest the time to find.

I will also tell you this: All of the best job search strategies and tactics in the world will not produce results unless an individual is properly disciplined and dedicated to see the process through. The challenge you have is in deciding which job search strategies and tactics are the best for the type of opportunities you want and then developing an organized job search campaign to find them. This book helps you deal with these challenges and more in direct and practical ways.

In this book you will learn how to:

- Work smarter; not harder.
- Create a job search marketing plan that attacks the need to find a position from several fronts.
- Understand that a targeted approach to finding a position is always better than using a scattered, shotgun approach.
- Develop the research skills necessary to search for and find a position to which you can then market yourself.
- Use a multitude of available resources (Web 2.0, business networking, direct marketing, etc.) to your greatest advantage.
- Relax and take some time to keep your health and sanity. Job search should be a balanced effort.
- Implement your plan, stay on the attack, and optimize your time and effort on a daily basis. Finding a job is much like a ground war: you have got to have a good plan of attack and be able to stay on mission until the objective is taken.
- Remain focused but flexible as you implement your job search marketing plan. The only thing that does not change is the fact that change is a constant.
- Learn and build positive momentum as you work your marketing plan. Every contact, every piece of data, and every idea you hear or see is an opportunity to learn and to add that learning to your arsenal of skills.
- Never blame your family, friends, the President, nature, or the economy for lack of results. You are entirely accountable for your success or failure during your job search.
- Help others along the way in their job search. Giving back to others by sharing your knowledge and insights will put you in a good place. Just do it.

As a part of the research for this book, I have included many of the interviews I conducted with experts from a variety of fields of interest, including networking, social networking, personal branding, communication, and recruitment. These interviews are designed to give you additional perspectives on issues that are critical to having an effective and successful job search campaign. They are noted in vignettes throughout this book as Expert Insights.

It is Not About the Résumé

There are a few things that I should point out that this book is purposely designed not to cover: One thing this book does not cover is how to shine your résumé or your shoes. There are already a multitude of great books on the subject of résumé writing (see the Resources section in Chapter 20). This book also will not tell you what to say during an interview. The simple truth is this: *Your résumé and shined up shoes will not do you much good in landing a job if you cannot find the right opportunities.*

It sometimes stuns me at just how people agonize and spend countless hours over their various résumé formats. Is a well-formatted résumé important? Yes. However, it will not find you a job. Blasting it out is a numbers game that does not yield positive returns. It only leads to frustration and dead ends.

Frustration and dead ends are not something you need during the course of a job search. This book is dedicated to avoiding that and keeping you focused on building a pipeline of job opportunities that others will not bother to find. Your journey of becoming your own personal marketing manager and positioning yourself to become an opportunity machine when the need arises begins right here.

David E. Dirks
July 2009

Chapter 2
The Rules for Job Search Success

Your Mission: To find job opportunities in the shortest amount of time possible.

Successful job search marketing results in you uncovering job opportunities that others will miss. Over time, I have learned that there are certain "rules of the road" that form the bedrock for the fundamentals that drive job search success. It is absolutely critical to grasp and understand these basic rules well before you undertake your job search campaign. Keep these rules in mind as you proceed to build your job search campaign and you will be rewarded with the results you need.

Rule #1: Start your job search marketing campaign immediately.

Whether you have been laid off or have decided to find another place to carry on your career, finding your next job opportunity is your top mission. Your goal is really two-fold: First, you want to find a good job that allows you to advance your career goals, and second, you want to find another position as quickly as possible. Sounds reasonable right? It is, and it should be an expectation regardless of what the current economy and the job market look like.

Too often, however, there are things that can get in the way of these goals. To be clear, there is no such thing as an "optimal" time for finding your next opportunity. It will vary based on factors outside of your control. In a vibrant economy and a healthy, fluid job market, it might take you a short amount of time to find your next position. Conversely, when the economy is down, it is reasonable to expect that it will take longer to find a job.

For example, if it takes the average person eight months to find a position, the goal is to reduce that by at least half that time or less. How is that possible? It is possible, if you focus on the right techniques. Most people waste a huge amount of time placing too much energy on the wrong elements of the job search. For example, what is the first thing you think about when someone is about to begin looking for a new job? The résumé! While certainly a key tool in the job search process, by itself it will not create opportunities. Many people just starting out in their search eat up valuable time and money agonizing about how their résumés should look.

For the average job searcher, the next step usually consists of combing the classifieds, checking out job databanks, contacting recruiters, and perhaps e-mailing a few people from personal networks. These are all good things to do but usually produce a dark hole. A dark hole, in job search terms, is an abundance of résumés in people's hands that yield few returns and have little impact on generating good leads.

This regimen becomes the daily grind for the average job searcher. Day after day of e-mails, Internet applications, reviewing the classifieds, contacting recruiters, and other such standard job search techniques often result in an empty silence, and no leads. Before too long, frustration can set in. You can get mighty discouraged by the silence and inactivity coming from your intensive, daily efforts.

So what can you do to avoid the pitfalls of the average job search? The first step is to not get lazy. The time to strike and start building your job search marketing strategy is immediately after you find out you are being laid off.

If you have been laid off and did not see it coming, it is understandable that you might be in shock for a day or two, but slap yourself

Job Search Marketing

out of that mode. Splash some cold water on your face because you are staring at the reality of your situation: you need to find another job, and you need to do it now.

Rule #2: Have a personal marketing plan that is integrated and coordinated.

Now that we have rule #1 clear, let's discuss the next critical area in your search, and that is making sure you are able to leverage all the job searching resources at your disposal today. Therein lies the next challenge you will have: creating and deploying an *integrated and coordinated* marketing plan. Notice the emphasis on the words *integrated* and *coordinated*. Many people of all levels of sophistication and business experience fail to recognize that a job search marketing plan that does not easily integrate and coordinate each resource, strategy, and tactic is bound to slow you down in your search. Your search marketing plan must create a very disciplined "harmony" and linkage between all the search efforts you make.

There is such a wide variety of resources, strategies, and tactics you can deploy in your search for a new position. Between the Web, networking tools, research tools, recruiters, and other resources, the amount of things you can do to accelerate your job creation is mind-boggling.

Just take a look at the number of business and social networking options you have these days. LinkedIn, Facebook, MySpace, Ning, and many more viable options for job search networking are available at your finger tips. Which ones are best for you? How do you deploy them for maximum effectiveness? Which ones are wastes of time? How much time should you allocate to them during the search process?

When creating your marketing plan, ask yourself these questions: What is the connection between your networking efforts and your database of contacts? How are you measuring success or progress towards your goals? What is the relationship between your per-

- 11 -

sonal branding efforts and your focus on generating viable job leads? How are your personal contacts linked to your job search? How do you divide and allocate your daily time to each strategy, tactic, and resource you want to take advantage of?

Rule #3: Stay focused and be sure to recharge your mental attitude often.

Another key point is to remain relentlessly focused on deploying your job search marketing plan on a daily basis. It is not unusual for many searchers to get highly motivated on the front end of the search and then, over time and after a bit of rejection, allow discouragement to settle in and slowly send the searcher's energy level plunging.

Discouragement is a job search killer, and it can happen either very quickly or very slowly over time. It all depends on your attitude. Discouragement is the number one killer of job search success for the simple reason that it can make you blind to employment opportunities. You will not see or react with the same level of sharpness and enthusiasm if you are discouraged and distracted during your search.

Rule #4: Stay grounded in reality from the beginning of your job search to the end.

Reality is often described as the perception that you have about any situation; hence, perception is reality. Perhaps that is so in some situations. For example, how you are perceived by your friends or your boss is often based on their perceptions of how you are. That means that people's knowledge of who you are is not always grounded in fact. Although it happens all the time, it is a dangerous game to let your perception of a potential employer or job opportunity get in the way of your ability to really assess it for what it is.

How many stories have you heard about people who, at the end of their search rope, decide to take just about any job that comes along at any reduced rate in salary? The perception might be that any job is better than no job except for the fact that you may lose on two levels. For one thing, a lower-paying job will most likely not keep you afloat financially for any length of time. For another, working in a dead end, lower-paying job means you lose focus on your true goals by having less dedicated time to allocate to your job search.

Rule #5: Take only a sharply targeted approach to your job search marketing.

We are a mass market kind of society and there are plenty of people who treat the job search process the same way. I can recall as a hiring manager myself, getting résumés from folks who had no business sending me one in the first place. A hiring manager should provide as specific as possible descriptions in the posted job opening about the key accountability points, minimum amount of experience necessary, and the baseline skills needed to be successful in the position. In many cases, the searcher is able to get that picture from most (but certainly not all) job postings. But listen to hiring managers or recruiters, and they will tell you that a large percentage, perhaps a third or more, of the résumés they receive are from people are not remotely qualified for the position.

Why is that? Answer: Mass market job searching has great appeal to those who think they should leave no stone unturned. This approach is the shotgun approach to marketing yourself to the world. The idea that you can blast your hard copy or e-mailed résumé to the world and expect any results is unrealistic. I have found that as the job search lingers on, panic can set in and the pressure to show results quickly forces some to carry out a mass market approach to their job search. It is busy work that generally leads to a dead end with more frustration and discouragement. This can lead to a downward spiral that can be totally debilitating to the job hunt.

Rule #6: Start and end your job search on the premise that there is a job out there with your name on it and your challenge is to simply find or create it.

When the economy gets tight and the media provide a daily deluge of negative information, it can be hard to see the light of opportunity. When large companies announce that they are laying off thousands employees and when friends and relatives laid off two years ago still cannot find work, it becomes easy to think that here are no jobs for you. No matter how bad the employment market is, there are still companies who are hiring. Your job is to seek them out and either find a position you are qualified for or create a job opportunity for yourself.

In tough economic times, media outlets would have you believe that, given the latest unemployment numbers, industries are only losing jobs, not creating them. In fact, every month, new jobs are created and current jobs need replacements. The number of new jobs created is often never reported until that number exceeds the job loss number and vise versa. When times are bad, all you hear about is how many jobs were lost. When times are good, you only hear about the jobs being created. Employment is rarely reported in the media in a balanced way. Ignore the numbers. Focus on being hired, not the unemployment numbers.

You need to believe that there are some job opportunities that need to be found and *others that need to be created*. Recognizing that you have the ability to *create* a job opportunity is not something most job seekers think about. If you can solve business challenges, you can create a job opportunity.

Rule #7: Be a helpful and valuable source of information and support to others who are conducting their own job searches.

This rule is probably the most important of all. It is a simple tenant that is based on your ability to help others in their job search efforts. Long ago, high-performance sales professionals learned that the best way to keep a customer is to help the customer in his business in any way possible, even well after the sale. These sales professionals send along information they know their clients can use to make their business better.

This principal applies to helping others who are in the same boat as you. Make it a point to consistently help others in their search efforts. For example, you might find a job that might be better suited to someone you know…send it to him. Or, you might find some networking opportunity that a friend could also take advantage of as well…share it with him. Helping others where you can add value to their search efforts builds goodwill that can often translate into reciprocal help for your own job search effort.

Develop a reputation for assisting others that you know who are also conducting a job search. Share information with them. Discuss some of your ideas, strategies, and job-search tactics. When appropriate, try to introduce them to people you know that might be able to help them. Expect nothing in return.

Chapter 3
The World of Job Search

Modern job search is not your father's job search. With sweeping changes occurring on a regular basis that affect how we conduct business these days, it is no wonder why many are frustrated with their job search results. The fact that a job search is not something you will find yourself doing very often makes it even more of a challenging issue. Perhaps only a handful of times over your working career will you need to conduct a search. Some people can go ten years or more and never have to worry about finding another job.

As a topic, job search is something that is talked about or thought about on a regular basis. So, when you find yourself needing to conduct a job search, it is easy to have a traditional reaction: immediately fix the résumé and start mailing, faxing, and e-mailing it out to the world.

In the old days, you could rely on recruiters, print advertising, employee referrals, and traditional "face-to-face" networking to provide you with a flow of potential job opportunities. Before the Web 1.0 and 2.0 came along, those approaches were the primary ways that businesses and prospective talent came together. However, advances in technology have expanded the frontier of finding career opportunities in ways no one could have thought possible ten or even five years ago.

The one thing that has never changed is that opportunities will not find you; you need to position yourself in such a way that you create natural conduits that allow for you to uncover opportunities that others never see or hear about. Web 2.0 has just simply given you additional tools that make finding an opportunity a much more time-effective process. Today, from the comfort of your home, you can literally search and make contact with the world.

The Résumé: Not the beginning but the end

Ask most people about the first thing they think of when considering their job search and they will most likely chat about their need to create or update their résumés.

The typical reaction for most job seekers is to send out as many résumés responding to as many job sources as possible. That leads to the "black hole résumé" syndrome. Résumés go into the hole but never come out. Your résumé gets stuck with hundreds, if not thousands, of other résumés and never sees the light of day.

A résumé is a nonliving, dead piece of material. It cannot magically find you a job. It cannot close the deal and get you to an offer. It cannot do much to keep you from getting a TBNT letter (that stands for "thanks but no thanks" and is a letter you will routinely see and get during a typical job search).

A résumé should never, ever, be sent out unless it is as a follow-up to a conversation (either verbal or e-mail) you have already had with a key decision maker or key influencer. A <u>key decision maker</u> is someone who can make a hiring decision. A <u>key influencer</u> is someone who can potentially connect you with a key decision maker.

If you follow this rule when sending out résumés, you will see that it leads to far greater results. This is a sales strategy right out of the best practices for top sales professionals. High-performing sales people sell on the basis of a relationship they have with their customers. They do not hide behind a marketing brochure and hope someone will call. The best skillfully locate their best prospects and engage them directly before sending a marketing brochure, if they send one at all. Top performing sales professionals do not sell brochures (read: résumés); rather, they sell themselves.

Most people get stuck on the idea that they have to take a mass market approach to job search. Send a cover letter and résumé to everyone and anyone that looks remotely like a job lead. Throw it on the wall and see what sticks and then find out that little actually does stick, if anything at all. These people have spun their wheels paying for valuable postage, copying, and time for stuffing the envelopes or e-mailing the résumé. The mass market approach might make them feel better in the short term, but, take my word for it, it will grind them down.

In your job search, consider the principal of less means more. Less paper shuffling and more focus on building relationships, locating key contacts, and then building quality relationships with them is not a mass market strategy. It is a one-to-one job search strategy.

The Constant Need for Talent

Whatever the health of the economy or job market is at any one time, there is one thing that stays constant: businesses will always need talented people. "Talent" is defined as people who are hired by a business to serve as the core foundation for growth, productivity, and profitability. I will say it again: In good times or bad, businesses always need talent.

It is essential to engage in an understanding of just how businesses go about finding the right talent. Understanding the talent acquisition process can help you during the course of developing and implementing your job search marketing plan. It is the kind of knowledge that can help you leverage your time and resources in powerful ways.

In 2008, the Newman Group (an independent survey company) polled 500 staffing professionals from businesses of all sizes and industries. The results of this poll exposed two interesting facts: First, when asked about the most challenging part of the hiring process, these staffing professionals sited sourcing qualified candidates. Second, and even more telling, was the fact that 68 percent of the respondents said that employee referrals were their most productive method for finding talent. This fact alone has incredible implications on your search. It should tell you two things: 1) your network of contacts from your previous employer are valuable even if you are not employed there anymore, and 2) that networking with certain employees of companies you may be targeting is a critical strategy for your job search.

Using online databases was cited by 78 percent of those surveyed as an effective strategy for locating talent. "This strong showing came as something of a surprise, simply because such searching requires significant effort from recruiters who are commonly overstretched in their current roles," noted the survey.

Most recruiters found that posting positions on job boards (such as Monster.com or hotjobs.com) are "somewhat effective" as a candidate sourcing tool. Why? Simply because most job posting sites have become places where you can generate lots of quantity but little quality in candidates. These mega job posting sites have become black holes that suck up torrents of candidate information and spit out torrents more but to less effect for both employer and prospective candidates.

Most recruiters have two choices in terms of how they recruit. First, they can use passive tactics, such as job postings or classified ads, and wait for the candidates to come to them. Or, they can proactively source by networking, using employee referral programs, campus recruiting, or searching online databases. Most businesses apply a combination of both tactics. However, in recent years, some businesses have begun to rely on singular approaches to hiring, such as only using Facebook as a social media database for connecting with prospective employees.

With speedy access to data that was once impossible to tap into, recruitment has become a knowledge-based process. "The knowledge-based approach to sourcing also includes use of Web 2.0 and social networking to actively reach out and *know more people* (emphasis is mine). It is a continuous and proactive approach. Recruiters cannot wait for the job to become open to start building a network of candidates....LinkedIn remains a leading source used by respondents, with 85 percent of respondents using it as a key sourcing tool," noted the Newman Survey. Linkedin is one of the leading online social networking platforms that are being used today by millions of professionals.

In another study, Jobvite (www.jobvite.com) conducted a social recruitment survey that looked at how employers sourced for candidates. Jobvite found that:

- 76 percent of employers surveyed plan to invest in employee referral networks
- 72 percent plan to increase their use of social networks for recruitment
- 66 percent have successfully hired a candidate identified or introduced through an online social network

Clearly, recruiters and companies of all sizes and industries have been changing the way they acquire talent for their organizations. The impact of these changes on the process of job search has been dramatic. However, when armed with the right blend of both traditional and nontraditional job search strategies and tactics, any job seeker can create a personalized job search marketing campaign that delivers the results. The result should be a steady stream of job opportunities that gives the job seeker a richer array of career options than most people think is possible.

Job Sourcing Tools

Let's take a quick survey of just some of the job sourcing tools you have at your disposal:

Print advertising: There is no question that there are less businesses willing to spend valuable dollars on expensive print ads today. You need to look no further than the incredibly shrinking amount of classified and display advertising sections in your local paper to find proof. Web 2.0 resources such as LinkedIn are quickly taking over this traditional candidate sourcing space.

Job fairs: Job fairs are a sourcing technique for businesses that are looking for passive ways to source for qualified candidates. General fairs are probably the least effective way to source qualified candidates. The recruiter cannot be assured that the next person they spend even three minutes with is qualified. The recruiter has to manually evaluate each person who steps up to the booth to determine if he is qualified or not. And it is not any more effective for the prospective candidate, either. Unless it is a targeted job fair (i.e., a job fair targeting jet engine mechanics), it is a mass market event and therefore too broad in scope to be an effective tool. A job fair's most redeeming quality is that it might be a great way to network with hiring managers or recruiters for companies on your target list.

Personal/professional contacts: The basis for any networking effort is your personal contacts. Friends, relatives, fellow employees, alumni associations, professional associations, and general business contacts are a strong foundation to get to know more people. Everyday there are people who find their next job from a referral or contact made on their behalf. Networking personal contacts has always been an effective way to find or create job opportunities.

Recruitment firms: When companies want to cut through the clutter and "sort the wheat from the chaff" to weed through candidates, they turn to recruitment or headhunting professionals. There are literally thousands of recruitment firms that cover the gamut of career fields and industries. The key to optimizing your results from a recruitment firm is based on how well you manage the relationship. Recruitment firms are still a viable resource for any job search campaign.

Job postings (Web-based): This tool cuts three ways. First, many companies have their own listing of current job openings on their Web sites. Then there are the mega job posting sites, such as Monster.com or hotjobs.com. There are hybrid job posting sites that aggregate job postings from other sites on the Web into one site (i.e., Indeed.com). However you slice it, job postings are generally electronic and remain an effective tool for sourcing opportunities.

Social networks: Facebook, MySpace, and LinkedIn are just a few of the many Web-based social sites that are available to search for hiring contacts and new job postings. These Web 2.0 tools have expanded the frontiers of traditional business socializing and networking by providing a quicker way to access information. Using these tools, you can reach out and connect with people who can help you expand your job search resources.

Viral networks: YouTube.com has become the poster child for the way to gain attention in a crowded job market by showcasing your expertise using a short and focused video clip. It is a mass market job search tool that must be carefully planned and executed in order to be of value to your job search efforts.

Online groups: Staying active during your search means finding online social networking groups related to your career interests from online aggregators such as Ning, MSN Groups, Yahoo!Groups, and GoogleGroups.

Cold calling: This approach is not for the feint of heart but clearly a job search tool that is mostly underutilized. Recruitment firms have long used the old-fashioned phonebook approach to sourcing candidates. A new recruiter would be given a desk, phone, and the latest copy of the business phonebook and begin dialing. The same applies for those looking for job opportunities.

News media scanning: Today, we have access to more media information than ever before. Both print and online versions of news outlets provide the job searcher with the ability to scan for news stories that might lead to finding a new job opportunity. Sometimes your next job is buried in the news.

Blogging: It was not long ago that few even knew what a blog was. Fewer still are able to grasp just how important blog can be to your job search process. A blog is simply an online journal where you can write about any number of topics. It is a great way to showcase your expertise and knowledge to the world.

Personal Web site: Like having a blog, having your own Web site that has been engineered for the purpose of helping you find your next job opportunity is key. What better way to help promote yourself and what you can do for a potential employer than by using a simple Web site to showcase your talents and expertise? In job search marketing, having your own Web site is a must.

E-mail marketing: Developing a viable and growing e-mail list of contacts that can help influence your success during your job search is an immediate priority. Creating a contact management plan that includes well-planned e-mail campaigns is the next priority. Providing potential job contacts with valuable information that can help them based on your area of expertise on a programmed basis can set you apart from the crowd.

Writing a book: Nothing says "expert" more than writing a legitimate book. Lots of people talk about writing a book on their area of expertise but very, very few actually have the focus and ambition to do it. There is a lot of work that goes into writing a book, which is why most people do not attempt it. You need to carefully consider the impact and value of writing and publishing a book against your available time. That said, if you decide to take on the challenge of writing a book related to your career field, it is certainly one way to clearly differentiate yourself from your competitors.

Consulting: There is no better way to network and find your next potential employer than by providing consulting services to that employer. If you are really good at what you do, then show that company your skills and earn some money at the same time.

Temporary services: Many employers use the temporary service firm as a way to find and screen potential employees. At the very least, finding out what companies are hiring temps may help you find those businesses in your area that are still healthy and looking for good talent.

Google and other search engines: Search engines are some of your most powerful allies in your job search marketing plan. Search engines such as Google are very popular but underutilized in the job search. While many people know how to conduct basic searches, few understand the finer points of researching techniques, like improving search results and using tools like Google Alerts to help you create a job research machine that works for you 24/7.

Corporate annual reports: Annual reports are easy to access and full of information and data that you can use to your advantage in your job search.

Outplacement Services: If your firm provides you with outplacement services as a part of your severance package, make full use of them. My observations with respect to outplacement firms is that most eligible employees don't take full advantage of them when they are offered. Most outplacement professionals will tell you that only a small percentage of eligible employees actually take advantage of the services provided. Of those that do, few of them stick with outplacement long enough to have it do any good.

Chapter 4
Your Marketability Assessment

Question: What Makes You a *Compelling* Job Candidate?

Compelling is defined as being forceful or demanding attention.

Instead of focusing on your résumé, start your job search by focusing on how marketable (read: compelling) you are as a job candidate. Here are the key questions you want to clarify, before you can create an effective job search campaign:

- What makes your experience valuable to any employer?
- What can you do that delivers the services that an employer actively needs/seeks?
- Why does hiring you make sense?
- What are the variables that differentiate you from your competitors?
- What can you do for a company that makes you a *compelling* candidate?

A marketability assessment should help you accomplish three things: 1) it should clarify and define what it is that you produce that makes you a valuable talent, 2) enable you to target only those opportunities that are within the scope of your talents, and 3) begin the process of helping you differentiate yourself and build a personal brand.

Your marketability assessment is the foundation for all your job search strategies and tactics going forward. If you can articulate what exactly it is that you can deliver to an employer, you will be well ahead of your peers. Answer that question now and it brings into line your ability to locate and target those opportunities that you are qualified for.

Your marketability as a candidate gives you what marketers commonly call your "competitive positioning." Knowing your competitive positioning is a key factor in your job search success. High performing marketers and sales people know their products inside and out. They know the benefits of their products and services so well that they can sell them with passion. They can 'evangelize' and inspire others to buy their products. This same business principal applies to your ability to 'know thyself' better than anyone else as it relates to your competitive positioning in the job market.

If you can clearly position yourself against a gaggle of other candidates, your chances of breaking through are better than average. But you cannot do that until you take inventory of your career experiences and understand how they translate into value for an employer.

If you get this part right, the rest of the process is much easier. If you get this wrong, you will always seem to be climbing a mountain. Why? If you can't articulate what your expertise is and how it adds value to any potential employer, it will affect your ability to position yourself in the best light during a job search campaign. For example, when you set up your networking account on LinkedIn, you have an opportunity to portray your work/career expertise, values, and your contributions in terms of results from your work. With a clear understanding of your competitive positioning (knowledge, skills, values, contributions) your LinkedIn profile will not be as effective as it can be.

After reviewing your LinkedIn profile, it should be pretty clear to the reader what your competitive positioning is. Otherwise, they'll skip your profile and start looking elsewhere.

The more you know about yourself as a professional in terms of the specific components of your competitive positioning, you'll be able to discern which job search strategies and tactics are best suited to your campaign.

In this next section, we'll take a deeper look into the process of inventorying your knowledge, skills, and contributions in the context of a job search campaign.

Step One: Inventory Your Knowledge (What do you know?)

Knowledge: the fact or condition of knowing something with famil-iarity gained through experience or association.

Taking inventory of your knowledge is a critical step. It requires you to make a list of the knowledge areas that you possess. Knowl-edge areas are the components, pieces that, when brought together, allow you to develop the skills that deliver tangible results.

For example, a builder may know how to build a house. Before he ever put a nail in a board, he has to first learn and master a body of knowledge. A builder has to have a body of knowledge built around construction design, blueprint reading, building materials, and the mathematical calculations necessary to improvise or modify the build-ing plans when necessary. He has to have knowledge of building ma-terials and construction techniques that are used with each phase of the building process, knowledge of project management and people management, and an understanding of pricing a project. There are lots of points of knowledge that a builder needs in order to be func-tional.

Try this exercise:

Find a quiet area and bring a blank pad & pencil with you. Brain-storm (jotting thoughts & ideas down without judging or editing them) each point of knowledge that you possess as a professional in your field. Remember, a point of knowledge is a specific body of knowledge that someone in your field has to possess in order to be effective. Think of points of knowledge as the 'book' knowledge you need to have as a foundation for developing skills.

Step Two: Inventory Your Skills (What can you do?)

The knowledge you possess translates into *actionable skills*. The better you understand the variety of ways your knowledge yields skills that you can apply to a job situation, the more effective you will be at marketing yourself during a job search.

You will frequently hear people say that knowledge is power. This is not so. Knowledge is not power. *Applied* knowledge is power. Knowledge that sits on the shelf is useless.

In the case of our builder, he has to take the body of knowledge he has and apply it directly to the process of building a home. A builder starts with raw land and begins to apply what he knows and shapes that knowledge into a home. In the process of building the house, he applies knowledge that translates into tangible skills.

An aircraft pilot has to do that same thing. Let's take a look.

The Power of Applying Knowledge and Creating Flight

A good friend of mine, Lt. Colonel Willie Biggin, flies the super-large military cargo plane, called the C5A, for the Air National Guard. I asked him what body of knowledge one might need to possess before he could even think of flying a plane like that or any jet engine aircraft for that matter. Here is some of what he told me:

A pilot must understand basic aerodynamics. "This covers what makes an airplane fly, the four forces on an airplane; lift, drag, weight, and thrust. While covering these areas, a pilot would need to understand how a wing or airfoil works. An emphasis would be put on how these relate to an airplane in flight."

A pilot must understand basic weather. "A basic knowledge of how the different types of weather can affect how the airplane will fly is critical to being a pilot."

A pilot must know the limitations of the airplane he is flying. "Whether it is weight, speed, or engine limits, a pilot must know what the limits are so that when he approaches them, corrective action can be taken so that the limitations are not exceeded. When limits are exceeded, bad things can happen."

A pilot needs to understand basic aircraft systems. "This includes the different systems which are unique to each airplane. This would include the engines, hydraulics, pneumatics, fuels, pressurization, electrics, and flight controls."

Even when you know all these things, you are still not ready until you have the opportunity to apply your basic flight knowledge to a real life situation. All these things are part of a pilot's basic foundation of knowledge. You have to know it but this knowledge will not get the plane in the air until it is applied.

Lt. Colonel Biggin gave two examples of where a pilot gets to apply his knowledge:

Basic instrument flying: "This training and knowledge gives the pilot the ability to fly in the clouds, rain, and fog, generally speaking. The pilot learns to fly by using his flight instruments, without looking out the window or being able to use outside references. This is an essential skill that must be learned and practiced to maintain currency but also a high degree of proficiency."

Situational awareness (SA): "There are many ways to describe SA, but I think of it as the pilot's ability to understand the current environ-

David E. Dirks

ment and be able to accurately anticipate what will happen next and take the correct appropriate action to safely operate the airplane during the flight. SA comes naturally to some pilots but is constantly developed in all pilots through increased knowledge in all areas related to flying and accumulation of flying experiences. To have good SA, a pilot would say that he is ahead of the airplane. But with SA that is lacking, he might be 'hanging on to the tail' or 'five miles behind the plane."

Whether pilot, builder, engineer, accountant, stockbroker, marketer, or sales professional, understanding the difference between knowledge and applied knowledge is critical to your job search. You need to understand what you know for sure but be able to articulate and define how your applied knowledge benefits a prospective employer.

Identifying Your Skills

For our purposes, a skill can be defined as the action of applying knowledge through practical application and experience that creates some kind of output (the things you do with what you know). Those who apply knowledge to a greater extent than others are usually the ones who are considered highly skilled at what they do. By continually applying their knowledge and learning from their experiences, their skills become refined. That refining of the skill set can translate into output that is of superior quality.

What are your skills? What can you *do*? Any prospective employer is much more concerned with what you can *do* with your knowledge than anything else. You have to be able to identify the specific skills you have and the benefits of those skills as applied in the workplace.

Step Three: Inventory Gaps (What you *do not* know and what you *cannot* do)

You really have to understand your area's of expertise in order to do much good during this step. It is tempting during the job search process to think we know it all or at least list it on our résumé that way.

- 32 -

The fact is, you have gaps in your knowledge base, experience, or skills set that you have to recognize as such. In most cases, it does not take long for a sharp employer to spot those gaps from a mile away.

For example, there are plenty of people who call themselves marketers, but do all marketers have the same skills? Not even close. Some marketers focus most of their knowledge and skills on direct mail marketing or print advertising. Many marketers only focus on Internet-based marketing. Anyone considering himself in the category of marketer would have draw the distinction between being an expert in direct mail marketing versus print advertising or direct response television.

Make a list of what knowledge you do not have and what skills you do not currently possess. This might seem trivial but it is, in fact, quite critical. Here is why:

It gives you a ready-made list of knowledge and skills you should consider acquiring during the time you are in you job search. Use this time as you prepare for your job search campaign to shore up knowledge and skills areas that will help you broaden your market appeal to employers.

Step Four: Separate the basic value from the higher value (What makes you different? What skills in your career do you excel at?)

What are the knowledge and skill sets in your industry/career that are considered basic, the must-have skills that are required to be successful? Those are what I call 'basic value' skills. These are skills that everyone in your field should possess in order to be effective and contributing to the organization they work for.

Now, what knowledge and skill sets are considered 'advanced' within your industry/career? These are usually a combination of higher learning and work experience. This list should identify those things that begin to separate you from your peers.

Separating basic knowledge and skills from the advanced skills you have in your field is key. As you begin to reflect and understand the differences between these skills, a clearer picture of your market differentiation emerges.

Market differentiation is how you set yourself apart in a positive light against your peers. The more you can differentiate yourself from the crowd, the more effective you will be in your job search.

Great sales professionals do not sell the features of a product or service. Great sales professionals sell *benefits*. In your job search, being able to articulate and project the benefits of what you create and produce as output (work) is what will give you an advantage in your job search efforts.

In any job market, your ability to make it very obvious that you are the candidate of choice is based on your ability to differentiate yourself from your competitors.

Step Five: Inventory the kinds of positions you should target (What is my dream job and what jobs am I qualified for?)

Based on what you know and your ability to apply it, you should also know what kinds of positions within your industry/career you should zero in on. If your dream job is to become a Las Vegas comedian but you are currently a chemical engineer, you need a different book than this one.

Try this exercise:

1. Write a one-paragraph description of your dream job. What kinds of things would you do in this job? Ask yourself what makes this dream job so compelling.

2. Make a list of the types of positions you should search for based on the compelling components of your dream job and your advanced

knowledge/skills. Are there some gaps in what you could do versus what you can do?

Take a very rifled approach to what positions you should search for. Do not look to search for and apply for any job that remotely seems to fit you. There are not enough hours in the day for that strategy, and you will end up frustrated and grinding yourself down.

Step Six: Describe your ideal employer. (Who do I want to work for?)

This is another important step in the process of clarifying and confirming what types of employers you should be targeting. What would you expect an employer to be able to give you in return for your skills (besides monetary compensation, which we know is important)? What are the characteristics of your ideal employer? Is he demanding and providing you with a challenging work environment? What work skills does he place a premium on? How would he treat you in the work environment? What industries would he be in?

Try this exercise: Write a one-paragraph description on what your ideal employer would look like.

Here is an example: *My ideal employer would create a work environment built on challenging assignments and mutual respect, and would actively encourage and support my professional growth while paying me a market wage or better.*

Knowing *who* you would like to work for helps you focus your initial search energy on finding those employers and searching for positions within them. This is an easier task when you are looking to work for a large and/or well-established firm. It is sometimes easier to assess a prospective employer when you get into the interview and can ask questions to find out more about the employer.

The idea here is to whittle down your search to focus initially on the best available employers for your career needs and wants.

Are you an SME?

I believe everyone is a subject matter expert (SME) in something. It may be expertise in developing rocket fuels or maintaining a public school; whatever your career vocation is does not matter as much as what you are an SME in. If you understand what your knowledge base, basic, and advanced skills sets are, you can probably articulate your specific field of expertise.

From a marketing point of view, establishing yourself as an SME is critical to your ability to differentiate yourself in a crowded market as well as to begin to establish a personal brand identity. Once you can clearly identify yourself as an SME in one or several subject areas, it becomes easier for you to clear the decks for a powerful job search plan.

Once you establish your area of expertise, you now have to sell it to prospective employers. Many networking experts recommend that you develop and use a thirty second "elevator speech" that clearly hits the highpoints of what you do. Drilling down to a thirty second elevator speech is made easier if you write out an answer to this question: What are the *compelling* reasons for someone to hire you?

Businesses do not hire people for what they know. *Businesses hire people for what they can do for them.*

Marketing yourself successfully translates into being able to clearly identify and articulate the most compelling things you bring to an employer on your first day of work. If you cannot do that clearly, then you will look and sound like everybody else. If you cannot find reasons why you offer greater value as an employee than the next candidate, you will get lost in the middle of the shuffle. It is a bad place to be in.

Once you have a clear understanding of what you know (your knowledge base) and what you can do with what you know (your skill base), you can begin to develop a job search plan.

Remember, knowledge is not power. Applied knowledge is power.

Chapter 5
Your Contact Management System

The foundation of your ability to drive your job search strategy will be built on how well you are able to build momentum via your network of contacts. You will be successful in great measure based on how well you *manage* your contacts. The goal during your job search is to build a networking machine that has the capacity and forward momentum to work on your behalf. The principals that are at work in contact management in a job search are the same that work in the business world. The people who are the best at producing results (sales) from their network on a consistent basis are also those that invest time in managing those contacts.

The Truth about Networking

Truth be told, most people are pretty awful at networking. I know that sounds harsh but it is every bit true. In this case, I am not talking about people being too shy or introverted or unable to put two words together. (Although those people exist, too!) You could have the most terrific personality for networking ever devised and you could literally stink at networking. There is a litmus test that most people never really grasp or even pass.

The real litmus test in business networking is your ability to turn contacts into relationships and relationships into business. Great networkers are not great because they have sparkling personalities: Networking greatness comes from closed business.

Here is a real life example of why most people earn failing grades when it comes to business networking: A good friend of mine is in the commercial lending business. He attends three or four networking events a week between Westchester and Manhattan. These are not rag-tag networking events. These are attended by the professionally well-heeled from the world of commercial real estate, finance, and business brokering.

During his mingling, meeting, and networking, he collects a business card from every person he speaks to. He also gives each person one of his business cards. At the end of each session, he typically has between twenty-five and fifty cards. He meets and talks to a lot of people at each session. At the end of the week, he has amassed somewhere between seventy-five and 150 business cards.

What does he do with these cards? Let's back up a bit. When he gets a card from someone, he asks the person if he can add him to his e-newsletter. Almost everyone says yes. When he gets to his office, he enters each card into his database, taking the time to put each contact into a category, such as commercial realtor, lender, etc.

Now comes the key part. He immediately sends out an e-mail to that contact he just met a few hours ago just as a follow-up to their initial meeting. It's the immediate follow-up from the networking event that makes a big difference in his results. Then, his regular updates to his contacts via e-mail keep the networking moving along.

Invariably, my friend in the commercial lending business gets two or three networking contacts that will call him directly about a deal they need help with. Many others will also reply to his e-mail.

Following his process, regularly following up with his growing contact group week after week, month after month yields him a significant number of deals for his sales pipeline. He closes business because of it. He passes the litmus test.

Now, here is why I say that most people are not effective networkers: Remember that my friend gives one of his business cards to everyone he meets. In a week's time, he distributes an average of fifty and 150 of his own business cards each week during networking events.

How many follow up *with him* within forty-eight hours? Almost none. How many follow up at all? Fewer than 2 percent. Essentially, most people go to business networking events to collect business cards and then leave the cards in a dark desk drawer never to be seen from again.

For all the networking that goes on today, there is little effort made to actively manage network contacts. Some people like networking as it fits their personalities, while some would rather not bother. Either way, it is the lack of follow-up that kills any positive momentum that comes out of meeting and greeting network contacts. In the networking world, idleness kills.

Your Contact Database: All Contacts Enter Here

The first thing you will need to do before you begin your job search is to determine what mechanism you want to use to capture your contact data. You will need some kind contact management software that allows you to enter all of your contact data as you begin to build your job search network. This is the part that most people would rather avoid doing. It is not the fun part of this task of finding your next job. The fun part might be in attending a networking event and meeting new people, especially those who could directly or indirectly help you during your job search. However, the real work begins when you come back home and enter into your database the valuable contact information you gained. This is the step that most people miss entirely. It takes discipline to enter new contacts as we develop them each day.

What are some basic elements in a contact management database? You can add as much data as you think you can learn about a person, but here are the basics data tabs you should have:

- First, last name
- Company name
- Type of industry
- Job title
- Full address
- Office phone
- Cell phone
- Fax number
- E-mail address
- Web site address
- Blog address
- Best time to contact
- How you can help them
- How they can help you
- General notes/observations

Over time, you can add more data points, but this is a good list to start with and will serve you well over time.

Creating a database where you can easily locate your network contacts and manage the information you gain from them to your advantage is your goal. Fortunately, there are lots of resources available for you to use that can help you input and manage your network contacts. Let's review just a few of them here.

Microsoft Excel

Contact management software can be expensive, but it does not have to be. If you have MS Excel loaded on you PC or Mac, you already have a powerful tool that can be customized to meet your specific needs. This program is great for organizing and sorting contacts, and it is relatively simple to learn. If you are not that Excel-oriented, you may want to find a friend who knows how to power up Excel and help you create the contact management database you need for your job search.

Microsoft Outlook

If you already have MS Outlook on your PC, then you have a ready-made contact manager in place. This program is excellent for customization and linking to calendars, action items, notes, etc. It also allows for you to customize the contact template to suit your specific needs. Overall, it is a solid platform for managing your contacts. If you own it already, you might as well use it.

Google Contacts

Within the Google's very popular e-mail application called Gmail, there lies a ready made contact management database that allows you some ability to input most basic information on your contacts. It allows you to organize your contacts into groups and customize your contact information. For a free contact management system, it is pretty good. You might want to think about setting up a Gmail account just for you job search and this would be a good place to start.

Apple Address Book

If you are a Mac user, you will appreciate the contact management capabilities built into the Apple address book, a free software that comes with the computer. Apple's address book creates a customized template for your contact management data and provides the ability to connect the user directly to e-mail from the address book. It is not very robust as a contact management software option, but the price is right and the software will get the job done.

JibberJobber.com

With JibberJobber.com, you probably have the best overall contact management software that is available for free. The Web site is specifically designed for career management and job searches. You can input your current contacts from any number of places, such as Gmail, Linkedin, etc. It has a robust contact page that allows you to capture a lot of rich data over time from your contacts. The premium package costs only a few bucks a month and allows for far greater storage options than you get as a free subscriber. The Web site also allows you to set network relationship goals and get job feeds from aggregators, such as Indeed.com.

ACT!

If you are willing and able to invest in some software that is powerful and full of special features, then take a hard look at ACT! Currently only available to PC-users, it is probably one of the best contact management packages you can buy. It has been on the market for many years and has supported more sales professionals than you can count. The program has just about every conceivable feature you could ask for and then some. The only draw back besides the price, which is a few hundred dollars, is that it takes some time to fully learn and master the program. Like with on all full-featured programs, most people only scratch the surface in terms of using most of the features. Overall, this is a great premium contact management system for the job searches and beyond.

Daylite

Daylite is a Mac-based contact management software that is full of special features, but at a reasonable price. It seamlessly links contact info with your calendar, reminders, action items, and projects.

Now Up to Date and Contact 5

Now Up to Date and Contact 5 is another great contact and calendar management program that is available for both Mac and Windows users. It is reasonably priced and full-featured. This software is another great option if you are willing to invest a few dollars into your future.

Regardless of what software you choose, in order to conduct a productive and successful job search, you will need a good database in which to store your contact information. A contact management system is one of those worthwhile investment tools that will outlive your job search. You will never be able to leverage and manage the contact information you have if you try to do it on scraps of paper or keep it all in your head.

Leveraging Your CMS for Maximum Effect

So what can and should you do with a contact management system (CMS) once you have it up and running?

1. As you meet new people along your networking trail, their information goes immediately into your CMS. At the end of every day, check to see if you have any new contacts that need to go in and/or if you have updated information on your contacts that needs to be changed. Do this every day without fail. It is critical to get into the habit of keeping your database up to date every day. Many people start off well in this area but can quickly fall behind if they miss a few days or more.

2. If you have an integrated CMS, you have the ability to keep yourself organized and on track. Nothing is worse during a job search than having something slip through the cracks. If you promised to follow up on something for a contact, then you better be sure to do it. Anything less begins to chip away at your personal brand (reputation), and that is a blemish you cannot afford to have at anytime in your career.

3. As you spend more time with your contacts and develop a relationship with them, you will be able to input additional information about them into your CMS. Over time you might learn their birth date, their chief hobbies, and what kinds of things tick them off. All this information is relationship-based and critical for you to notate in your CMS. Think of it as building a file of information on someone. As you

get to know the person, you learn more about his history as well as his current situation. Instead of just nodding your head when you hear of new information (such as "I am really into restoring cars" and other such tidbits), you can make sure that data finds its way into your CMS.

4. Remember, knowledge is not power but, rather, applied knowledge is power. As your contact management system (or database) becomes more robust with information, it needs to be leveraged.

For example, say you have a new contact, and it is a recruiter you have recently met. Here is what you do from there:

- You exchange business cards and enter the contact into your CMS as soon as you can.

- Within twenty-four hours of meeting the person, fire off an e-mail that recaps your brief meeting and any follow-ups to each other.

- Add the contact to your monthly e-mail distribution list.

- Look the person up on his company Web site and scan for any other additional information that might be of value down the road. Log information such as what recruitment specialties he has; schools and organizations he belongs to; recent speaking engagements; books or articles he might have published, etc. Scan both the company Web site and a search engine (Google, for example) for more information on the person. Is he on Facebook? LinkedIn? MySpace? It is your job to learn as much as you can about each contact you meet and to add this information to your CMS.

- If you find the contact is on other Web 2.0 networking tools, such as Facebook or Linkedin, make sure you invite the person to link with you on those sites, as well. Do this within forty-eight hours of meeting the person while your meeting is still fresh in everyone's mind.

- Based on the information you accumulate on a contact, ask yourself these key questions:

1. What can I learn from the information I have on the person already?
2. How can any of that data help me to make contact and network with other recruiters?
3. If the contact belongs to certain associations, how can I leverage those associations to help me to directly or indirectly connect with potential leads/sources for job opportunities?
4. How might I be helpful to this person? Do I have information that might be valuable to him?

Always keep in mind that the whole purpose for investing time in setting up a contact management system is to leverage the information you gather to help you identify and get in front of job opportunities.

It is great to have an updated pile of contact information, but if you do not proactively use that information to leverage in your job search campaign, you have gained little. Many people enjoy the networking part of the content management process but loathe the work it takes to create a powerful database of contacts. If you develop, maintain, and leverage your CMS, you will be far ahead of your competition.

Asking for Referrals 24/7

If you invest the time to create and maintain a contact management system, your priority is to feed the beast you have created. This means that you have to leverage every opportunity to your advantage. For example, when you have a phone conversation or meeting with a business contact, that is an opportunity to ask if the contact knows of anyone who could help you in your search. If asked, most people are more than willing to look through their rolodexes to scan for anyone who might be able to help you.

'Help' comes in two flavors here: direct help, which is where you meet someone who has hiring authority and can directly influence the outcome of a job search, and indirect help, which is simply defined as when you make contact with someone who can connect you with people who have direct hiring authority.

Just think about this: If you asked everyone you know for three contacts that could directly or indirectly help you with your job search, you would probably get a bunch of new contacts to connect and network with. How many people do you know? I will bet you know more people than you think.

Let us say you know one hundred people, which includes friends, relatives, and business contacts. You ask each to help you by providing additional networking contacts. If only half of them respond, you would still end up with between fifty and 150 new people to add to you contact base. Surely, not all can be helpful but at the very least, these new contacts might put you in touch with someone who can help. It is kind of a multiplier effect. Each time you meet someone, that one person puts you in contact with more people. The combination of expanding your contact database and then actually using the contact data is a very powerful combination indeed.

One of your most important tasks during your job search is to make sure you always have a flow of new network contacts to keep your CMS healthy and growing. The second most important task is to leverage your CMS by staying in contact with your network on a regular and consistent basis.

Chapter 6
Job Search & E-mail Marketing

As your contact management system grows over time with more contacts, you will need to stay in touch with these contacts on a regular and consistent basis. E-mail marketing to your contact database allows you to develop and maintain a cost-effective relationship on a regular basis. In addition to direct mail, many successful companies today use e-mail marketing as a way to reach their customers and prospective customers in a moments notice. You should do the same with your contacts. If done correctly and within the parameters of the law, e-mail marketing will allow you to reach more people in a few minutes than you could reach by phone in several months' time.

Let it be said here: E-mail marketing is not a cure-all and should never be used in a vacuum. By itself, e-mail marketing has its limitations. For example, people of all kinds are bombarded constantly with junk e-mails that are clearly unsolicited. Any marketing medium can get tired quickly if overused. E-mail "fatigue" can set in if you blast e-mails on a too frequent basis or target people who have no business getting your e-mails in the first place. E-mailing your job search contact list is not a replacement for good old-fashioned networking by phone or in-person. E-mail marketing is always more effective when you use it in conjunction with phone and in-person meetings.

E-mail marketing can help you in getting the word out about your availability and help you expand your personal brand. While it does not match the power of the telephone call or the face-to-face meeting, it can do what those two items cannot: get information out to a large and targeted group of people faster.

What needs to be e-mailed? In Chapter 11, we cover the tactics that involve e-mail support such as announcing résumé updates, newsletters, updates to your personal Web site, new blog postings, new podcasts, etc.

Leap Frog Interactive on Best E-mail Marketing Practices

(Provided with permission from www.leapfroginteractive.com)

Like any form of interactive marketing, e-mail campaigns have particular strategies and decorum that are necessary to assure the most successful marketing effort possible.

- Do not use deceptive subject lines. Be sure the subject line is concise and pertains to what the e-mail is offering while providing enough relevant information to entice the recipient to actually open it.

- The e-mail's "from" line needs to clearly identify who sent the e-mail. The "from" line needs to be consistent in all the brand's e-mails so that recipients will easily recognize them each time they arrive.

- Recipients tend to respond to HTML e-mails the best. Using only text may help avoid spam filtering and be supported by all Internet users, but it is not as appealing. A balance between the two styles needs to be achieved. Simple messages will be able to deliver with great frequency than overly detailed and complexly designed e-mails.

- It is a good practice for a brand (meaning *you*) to include its name and a valid mailing address included in the body of the e-mail.

- Include a method for your contacts to use to opt out of receiving anymore of the e-mails. Be sure this feature, like an opt-out link for example, is valid up to thirty days after the e-mail is sent.

- If any mailings have been sent to your contact list before, remove "opt-out" contacts prior to sending a new message.

- The closing of an e-mail message needs to contain contact information, including physical address, and opt out information to comply with SPAM legislation requirements.

Let me give you some examples of how e-mail marketing can be leveraged during your job search campaign:

1. E-mail can be used to broadcast the launch of your initial campaign. If you do not have a lot of business networking contacts built up yet, no problem. Your very first job search e-mail should be to all of your personal contacts, including family. You should not pre-determine whether someone is or is not able or willing to help you in your search campaign. Some things that should be threaded into this kind of launch e-mail include:

- Tell contacts straight up what has happened to you (in the case of you losing your position due to a layoff). You may even want to announce it in the subject area on the e-mail. Here is an example of a good subject heading: *Dirks Job Search...Need Your Help!*

- Tell contacts what you need. Be as specific as possible as to the ways they might be able to help you. For example, ask them to introduce you to or forward contact information for people they might know who could be helpful in your job search specific to your career field and the types of jobs you are targeting. You should also be specific as to the companies you are targeting in your job search campaign and ask them if they have contacts or know of someone who has contacts at those firms. Bullet point out each type of information and/or contact you need so that it is easier for your e-mail recipients to figure out how they can help you.

- Ask them if they would be willing to forward your e-mail to people within their e-mail address book. This is a very powerful way to expand your e-mail impact. If you know one hundred people and your contacts each know one hundred people, then you have the potential to expand this kind of broadcast e-mail to a much larger audience. Some people will be happy to do that and some just will not. Any incremental expansion of your e-mail is a win.

- Be sure you include all of your contact information in the e-mail, so that it is easy for anyone who receives your e-mail to contact you. Some will e-mail you back and some will want to call you directly.

- To make this initial broadcast e-mail for your job search campaign most effective, make it a point to call each person you e-mailed a few days after you send it. Let the contacts know in the text of your e-mail that you will be calling them as a follow-up. This kind of follow-up is critical, especially in the context of announcing your job search to your e-mail address book of contacts. If you understand that most people these days have the attention span of a gnat, you will understand the need to reinforce your request for their help. There will be a good percentage of people who have information that could help you in your job search but they forget to respond to your e-mail. Calling them a within seventy-two hours after you have sent it will allow you to pick up information from those who could not respond to your e-mail request.

- Let contacts know you are willing and able to help them as well. It is good business to let people know that you understand that providing help is a two-way street. You need to be as willing and able to help someone with something as you want him to help you.

- At the end of the e-mail (and all subsequent e-mails of this type), make sure you thank the readers in advance for their "time and consideration."

- If you have a large e-mail address list (i.e., several hundred contacts) then you should consider resending the e-mail again within seven to ten days.

2. Use e-mail to update your contact list with newsworthy or "PR" information. You do not want to e-mail people just to remind them to help you. That will get your e-mail tuned out and rejected. Instead, use e-mail marketing to advice your contacts about things like a new newsletters, podcasts, YouTube postings, blog updates, and even new information and/or job search resources you found exceptionally helpful that you want to pass along.

Using e-mail to expand and deepen your job search campaign is an essential piece of your strategy. If used effectively, e-mail marketing can extend your reach far beyond what you could attempt to do via other communication tools. The key is to be selective in how you use it within you job search and to utilize it with enough regularity that it becomes an integrated part of your search process.
Note: This section is primarily for those who have lost their position through layoffs, etc. If you are gainfully employed, you have to obviously think through the idea of using e-mail marketing to announce you are looking for another job! It might not be a good idea but you are the judge of that.

Chapter 7
Job Search Networking 101

One of the most powerful tools you have in your job search arsenal is your ability to network and connect with other people. Networking is not anything new, but it is one of those areas that keeps expanding all the time. For many years, business networking was limited primarily to Chamber of Commerce events, tradeshows, association meetings, business clubs, company meetings, golf outings, and even personal events such as weddings.

Today, those are still great places to conduct business networking, but the web has provided a way to network that is far more powerful. Networking within the Web 2.0 world allows you faster access to new people and takes off the geographic limitations associated with traditional networking by allowing you to network around the world. By throwing off the shackles of space and time, the new age of business networking via the Web has also spawned a whole industry of book authors, workshop providers, business networks, and consultants.

If you are already used to attending networking events and meeting new contacts, you are ahead of the game and well ahead of your fellow job competitors. For some, networking is like punishment and only done when they absolutely have to. Get over it, and quickly. Everyone has his own personality and style. That kind of individuality is what makes networking so dynamic. The power of making connections is what makes networking such a great tool for you to employ during a job search. Put it this way, if you are not networking to some degree on a regular and consistent basis, your job search efforts will suffer greatly.

Here is a critical and universal rule with networking that you never want to break: Key in on how you can help your contacts. Networking is a two-way street, and you should always be thinking of ways you can help your contacts as you learn more about them, their needs, and their wants. People who engage in "one-way" networking are only fooling themselves. Skilled business networkers can smell from a mile away a phony person who is only looking out for him or herself. These one-way networkers get labeled as such and earn a reputation that completely tarnishes their ability to develop business relationships. Make it your business to help others, and they will be much more inclined to help you.

Here are some ways you can be tuned into helpful networking:

1. Listen more than you talk. Overcome the temptation to chatter on endlessly. Take a breath and let the other person talk. If you already listen more than you talk, you are way ahead of your peers!

2. Ask good questions. How is business? What is the person's greatest challenge? What interests does the person have? Ask questions that will lead to you discovering things that you can do to help the person in some way. Ask questions that signal to the other person that you are actually interested in what he has to say.

For example, say you find out that one of your contacts is trying to find someone to help him sell his business. You happen to know of a highly regarded business broker, and you refer this broker to your contact. Whether the two end up doing business is not the point. It is the fact that you reached out to help your contact.

3. Another thing to do as you get to know a person is to send the person relevant articles or Web links that you know would be helpful to him. There is nothing more powerful for business networking than when you send someone a handwritten note with a copy of a relevant news article inside.

4. Be consistent, dependable, and true to your word. Your bond is your word at any time, job search or not. Only promise when you know you can deliver. Set expectations with your network contacts so they are clear about what you can and cannot do for them.

5. Do not expect anything in return. Highly-effective networkers understand this principal well. Networking is not the quid pro quo process that some think it is. You just focus on being as helpful as you can. Avoid getting caught in the trap of thinking you deserve reciprocal help; it will kill your effectiveness.

When the time comes for you to need some advice or help, it will be there in spades. That is the power of networking.

Who do you know and network with already? Answer: A lot more people than you think!

Everybody knows somebody, and that is the first part of the exercise below. The moment you finish setting up your contact management system, you will want to do the following:

1. Make a list of everyone you know (and I mean everyone), including your mother. Sit down with a blank sheet of paper or two and just make a list. Do not edit it. You will have time for that later.

2. Next, sort your list into groups. Some basic categories would include personal (just friends, relatives), business, and any special groups, such as if you belong to an association or trade group. Do not go crazy here, but do make an effort to keep your contact list separated by groups that make sense and would be used for different purposes within your job search campaign.

For example, you might want to differentiate your business contacts that have direct hiring ability from your relatives. You also might want to have a separate group for recruitment contacts. This is particularly important as you organize or re-organize your e-mail groups.

There may be some things you will want to send to some groups but not others.

3. Be sure you have updated information on each contact. Phone, address, e-mail, Web site, work title, and company are the essentials you must have updated at all times. If you do not keep your contact information fresh, it will rapidly decrease in its ability to help you during your job search.

Not All Contacts Are the Same

There is another essential element to managing contacts, and it is simply this: Your contacts should not be weighted the same in terms of their relevance to your job search campaign. Think of each contact in the context of how relevant he is to your search (a key management contact versus Uncle Ned) and whether he is willing or able to help you.

Over time, you will learn that some contacts are more valuable and helpful than others. That is why you should establish a simple rating system that allows you to score your contacts in a way that gives you the ability to spend more time with contacts that are more relevant to your job search. With a finite amount of hours to work with during a search, prioritizing your contacts allows you to spend your networking time more effectively with those who can directly or indirectly assist you.

Here is a simple way to rate your contacts using a letter grade system.

Rating	Definition
A	Relevant to job search and willing to help you
B	Relevant to job search and not willing to help you
C	Not relevant to job search and willing to help
D	Not relevant to job search and not willing to help

Obviously, priority is always given to those in the A category, and for good reason. Your networking objective is to make contact and network with as many of these people as possible. These are the people who can either hire you or are very close to someone who can. These folks are the influencers within the business world who have the ability to provide you with some meaningful ways to find new career opportunities.

Contacts who have a B status are those you know who can help you in your job search but are unwilling to help you. Follow the old adage that you should "be nice to the people on your way up, as they are the same people you will meet on the way down." You might have a few people who are never going to help you no matter what you say or do. In the long run, you would hope to convert as many of these B contacts into productive contacts who want to help you where they can.

C level contacts might not be directly relevant to your job search in that they might not be in hiring authority and/or are well out of your industry networking circle. However, these are people who might just meet someone who could become a valuable contact for your job search. Your strategy here is to keep in contact with these folks. Drop them an e-mail every now and then to let them know how you are doing on your job search. Keep just enough contact with them to make sure they remember you and your need. Always ask them if they know of anyone or anything that might help you in your search efforts.

The last group, the D level is a group that, unless things change with them, there is not much to justify spending much time on them at all. The exercise here is to make sure you weed these people out of your active networking efforts and spend time developing relationships with higher quality contacts. Do not invest much or any time here.

Getting Closer to Your Targeted Employers

There is another way to look at how to evaluate networking contacts, and it is built on the premise that you can network with those associated with your targeted employers of choice (see Chapter 13—Developing Your Job Search Strategy). Here is a simple rating system based on a contact's ability to help you network within a targeted employer:

A: People who have relationships with key decision makers and who knows the company.

B: People who know the targeted company but have no relationships with key decision markers or anyone in the organization.

C: People who have a relationship with key decision makers but have no knowledge of the organization.

D: People who have no relationships within the company and have little to no knowledge of it.

Clearly, people who are in groups A and C are the ones you want to spend more time with. If you have contacts in those two categories, there are a few things you need to keep in mind:

1. Be honest and direct about what information you need from these people. Once you identify the people, your next objective to let them know you are in a job search. Then, ask them if they could refer you to people who might be able to help you or at least point you in the right direction within the company. If you do not ask, you will never know.

2. As you meet or connect with people within your targeted employer group, make sure you put them and their data into your contact management system.

3. If possible, make it a point to meet with key contacts on the basis of either a position they have open or, in the case they do not, meet with them at short meetings to get their insights on key issues facing the industry.

4. Be sure you follow through with anything you committed to during your meeting or phone call. Do not promise something you cannot deliver on.

5. Find ways to help your contacts. This is a great opportunity to send them copies of newspaper or magazine articles that you know they will appreciate. It is also a great way to make sure you are "top of mind" in their eyes. No need to send something every week but at least once a month or so is a great way to stay relevant.

6. Always send contacts a handwritten thank you note, especially if your contact took time out of his busy day to see you. It is a powerful yet simple way to differentiate yourself from your competition (who, by the way, will not remember to send a thank-you).

The intent of evaluating and rating network contacts is to help you focus your limited time on those who can help you in your job search campaign. When your contact database is small, this might not seem like a big deal. However, as your network grows, you will understand the need for a more disciplined approach to managing your contacts. Focus your efforts on growing those groups of contacts who have the ability to help contribute additional insights and hopefully more contacts for your job search campaign.

Chapter 8
The Face of Networking: Traditional Face-to-Face

Networking is not some new art form that was just invented yesterday. Networking has been around since the beginning of man. Over the years, many networking events, groups, and places have proven themselves to be tried and true. Let's just take a quick inventory and review a few of them that should be in your consideration set for expanding your own network of contacts.

College/University Alumni Associations

Almost every college has an alumni association attached to it. If you are not already a member of your college alumni, now is a really good time to join and get active. It does not matter if you are living close to your alumni college or not. The important thing is that you focus on connecting and reconnecting with alumni not only from your graduating class, but also those alumni that came before and after you. Alumni associations by and large have been vastly underutilized from a job search campaign point of view.

Web 2.0+ networking places, such as LinkedIn and Facebook, have a large number of alumni associations in which you can join. This is another way to ensure that you have leveraged your alumni power and have harnessed it to help you identify new job opportunities.

Tradeshows

Tradeshows come in all shapes and sizes. Almost every industry has tradeshows that are conducted annually. Tradeshows can be found on the local, regional, and national level, and you can find them held throughout the year. Find out what tradeshows are applicable to you and your job search interests. It does not take much of a Google search or a couple of visits to some industry Web sites to turn up relevant tradeshows. Tradeshows offer you an excellent opportunity to expand your network of job search contacts.

Here are a few guidelines you might consider when leveraging tradeshows for your job search campaign:

1. Attending larger, national tradeshows gives you a much bigger networking arena. In most cases, you will likely have to travel to attend a national show. If you can afford the expense and have excellent networking skills already, strongly consider it. However, if you are new to the tradeshow scene and are not yet confident of your networking skills, try attending smaller, more local shows to hone your skills and build your network. Start with local or regional tradeshows first, especially if you are new to attending tradeshows.

2. Your tool kit for tradeshow networking should consist of a notebook, personal digital assistant (such as Apple's iTouch), and business cards.

3. Always check to see if the people you meet at tradeshows are already on social networking sites, such as LinkedIn, Facebook, or other such sites.

4. Do not bring your résumé and do not parade the fact that you are out of work. It is not a good look at a tradeshow. Remember, this is different than a job fair. It's a tradeshow where people are trying to conduct business. Your business is to meet as many people as possible and get their business card data. Expand your contact management database today, and leverage the contacts tomorrow (after you get home).

Treat a tradeshow as a place for meeting people and making new contacts. Then get out. Here is the one exception: if you are asked during the course of a conversation what line of work you are in, by all means let them know you are seeking career opportunities. Ask them if they can help by referring you to others they know.

5. Dress appropriately for the show. You would think this would be a moot point, but more people than you think show up at tradeshows wearing shorts, flip flops, and other inappropriate clothing. Remember that you should dress to match the feel of the show. Be sure you know the dress code before you attend a tradeshow and then adhere to it.

6. Your objective is to meet as many people as possible and collect as many business cards as possible. Tradeshows are great places to meet new business contacts but do not get stuck with just one contact, unless there is a really good reason for it. Introduce yourself and get the business card information. Then move on.

7. Ask good questions. Ask your new contacts about the industry and what their opinions are of any pertinent issues. People like to share their expertise, so be sure you give them a chance. Just do not over do it. Remember, they are there to make contacts, too.

8. If the vendor is busy with a customer, move on and come back later.

9. As discussed in Chapter 5, Your Contact Management System, be sure you follow-up with each of the contacts you meet at a tradeshow within forty-eight hours. Get the contact's information into your contact database, and then send him an e-mail touching base and reminding him of your meeting. This would be a great time to let the contact know that you are looking for career opportunities and to ask him if he has any information (like other contacts) who may be of assistance. Be sure you evaluate the contact with your rating system and put each contact into the right group. Stay in touch with the contact

but do not stalk him. It is a good idea to always let your contact know whether you will be touching base on a monthly, bi-monthly, or quarterly basis.

Tradeshows are a great way to network and are especially critical during a job search. Find shows that work for you and attend them.

Chamber of Commerce Events

Chambers of Commerce have a long and well-established history for business networking. Many local and regional businesses become members of the local Chamber in order to make new contacts and build new business relationships. You can generally attend networking events sponsored by the Chamber without necessarily becoming a member.

Here are a few guidelines to think about when using Chamber events for networking.

1. Be very picky about the Chamber events you attend. My advice is to only attend those functions that allow you to work a room, meet people, and gather business cards. Remember, you are not attending these events to meet your next best friend. You are there to meet people you would not ordinarily get the chance to meet.

2. Have a short and concise "thirty second elevator speech". At most Chamber events, you will be asked about your career. Have a good answer, and be quick about it. Do not drag that opportunity out.

For example, here is one take on this scenario:

New contact: 'So, what do you do for a living?"
You: "I am in the (you name it) industry. Right now I am looking for new projects or job opportunities."
New contact: "I see. What did you do in your last assignment?"
You: "I had a very successful career as a (insert your career name here) for (name of company). Are you familiar with the industry?"

If the answer to that question is yes, then:
You: "Would you happen to have some contacts within the industry that I could talk to?"
You: "What do you do for a living?"

The key with the thirty second elevator speech is to keep it simple and make sure it is much less than thirty seconds in length. You will note that this quick introductory speech is a two-way conversation. Ask your contact if he is familiar with your industry, your previous company, and or might have any contacts within the industry already.

The idea in a Chamber networking environment is to give your new contact an idea of what you do while leaving out your entire biography. Some people are just bent on telling you the unabridged version of their lives and/or career. Do not be one of those people. Get your new contact engaged in the conversation as well.

Here are some basic rules of thumb when creating your thirty second elevator speech:

1. Tailor it to your audience and prepare it in advance of the event you are attending. What kinds of people will you have a chance to meet? Do they have a similar background as yours? Or are they part of different industries or businesses? You need to consider what types of people you will be in front of and make sure your thirty-second speech is geared to them.

2. The first sentence out of your mouth is the hook. What you say in the first few seconds determines whether or not your listener will tune in for the rest of your message. What can you say that can catch their attention? In the context of a job search, what is your most pressing issue or challenge?

3. Know what you want to accomplish in thirty seconds. Be as concise as possible. What is the question you want to answer? Limit and narrow your objective. Trying to get your life and/or career story

into a conversation usually results in you talking too much and your listener trying to figure out how to get away from you.

For example, let's say I am attending business networking events with the intention of expanding the number of business contacts for my job search network. Since my goal is to add as many new contacts to my network at the end of the event as possible, then my hook might be built around that theme. One potential hook is this: "I'm going to make the *Guinness Book of Records* with the largest business network in the world." (And said with a big smile on my face.)

The hook here is designed to be dramatic and sets the person up for my next request: "Can I have your business card to add to my network?" Be sure your hook gets the person's attention and keeps him interested in the rest of your thirty second speech.

4. For the meat of your thirty second speech, answer the question you proposed on step three. Using my last example, I might respond with: "I want to build the largest network in the world because I have just launched the largest job search campaign of my life!" I should give a short overview of my career field and then I should get the person's business card and ask him if he might know of someone who could help me identify job opportunities or potential network contacts. Then I am done. The thirty second elevator speech is done and the conversation continues through its natural course.

5. Practice, practice, practice. You need to practice your thirty second elevator speech before you hit the road. You only have one chance to make a positive and lasting impression upon someone when meeting them for the first time. Do not take it for granted that you will be able to "wing it" when you get to your event. The time to practice your thirty second elevator speech is not at the event. That is a price you cannot afford to pay during a job search campaign. You never know who you are going to meet and should assume that everyone you meet could be vital to your job search.

A well-honed, practiced, and smoothly delivered thirty second elevator speech allows you to be more effective during networking and other events during the course of your job search campaign. It also makes you more efficient and lets you cover more contacts.

Expert Insights with John D'Ambrosio and Dan O'Brien of the Orange County Chamber of Commerce

Dr. John D'Ambrosio is the President of the Orange County Chamber of Commerce in New York State since 1982. The Orange County Chamber is the largest business and professional organization in the Hudson Valley, New York, area with more than 2,300 members.

Dan O'Brien is the Senior Vice President of Membership Development for the Orange County Chamber since 1990.

You can find the Orange County Chamber at www.orangeny.com.

Dirks: In the context of conducting a job search, how can attending Chamber networking events help the person who is conducting a job search campaign?

D'Ambrosio/O'Brien:
- Allows him to practice presenting himself professionally.
- Allows him to meet potential employers and get his name known.
- Allows him to assess the competition.
- Allows him to find out who the appropriate contact person is at the company to which he may want to apply for a position.
- Allows him to learn about the experiences of others.

Dirks: What kinds of Chamber-sponsored networking events are best suited for the professional who is looking to meet potential contacts who could directly or indirectly help him with his job search?

D'Ambrosio/O'Brien:

- Monthly breakfast meetings, where the decision-makers gather.
- Tradeshows (for example, EXPOs, and Chamber-sponsored "Buy Local" Showcases).
- Any networking event (business networking blasts, seminars, mixers, etc.) can help indirectly.
- SCORE Counselors to America's Small Business. Make an appointment through the Chamber for one-on-one counseling.

Dirks: How would you recommend someone approach and work a Chamber networking event? What are some key do's and do nots?

D'Ambrosio/O'Brien:
- Monthly breakfast meetings, where the decision-makers gather.
- Smile.
- Introduce yourself (do not use titles) and extend your hand.
- Ask questions before talking about yourself and listen to the answers.
- Have a résumé to give to someone if the person asks for it.
- Do not talk with anyone for more than five minutes (unless it is obvious that this conversation is leading to possible employment).
- Do not spend your time at the event chatting with friends.
- Do not sit down or stay in one place in the room; keep moving.
- If possible, find out who will be at the event before you go.
- Ask the person you are talking to if he knows of an employer who may be looking for someone with your qualifications.

Dirks: For someone who is new to the world of networking, what skills does he need to have in order to network effectively?

D'Ambrosio/O'Brien:
- Appropriate speaking skills
- Good listening skills
- The ability to make the other person feel as though he is the only thing that matters at that point in time.
- Look people in the eye as he speaks, not over his shoulder or at the floor.
- Cultivate a pleasant personality
- Develop and use good follow-up skills.
- Be brave; do not take rejection personally.
- At the conclusion of the discussion, thank the contacts with whom the person speaks.
- Be aware of appropriate body language.
- Use a name tag if provided with one.

Dirks: What are five common mistakes you see people make when networking and how could they correct them?

D'Ambrosio/O'Brien:
- Dressing inappropriately or nonprofessionally.
- Talking more about yourself and what you want, rather than expressing interest in the other person.
- Looking over someone's shoulder (or anywhere other than the person's eyes) as you are talking with the person.
- Doing "hit and run" conversations throughout the networking event just to collect business cards.
- Sitting down or becoming rooted in one location throughout the networking event.

Dirks: Do you have any other comments/suggestions for the person who is undertaking a job search campaign as it relates to leveraging business networking?

D'Ambrosio/O'Brien:

- Treat everyday contacts as networking opportunities (i.e., talk to your physician, your hairdresser, the person in line with you at the grocery store, etc.). If nothing else, it gives you good practice at networking and interacting with people (skills you will need in any position). Be sure that all of your friends and relatives know of your job search.
- Stay abreast of what is happening in your areas of expertise (and business in general) so that you are prepared for intelligent conversations when you are in networking situations.
- Do not give up; use rejection as a learning experience.
- Do not forget that you are selling yourself; this is often more difficult than selling anything else.
- Remember the wise saying: "When opportunity knocked, I opened the door."

Economic Development Groups

Outside of your local Chamber of Commerce, there is another group that wields great power but is less well known. Most counties or regions have what is called an economic development corporation. These corporations are nonprofit organizations that are solely focused on marketing their respective geographies directly to companies looking to expand their business. For the most part, this marketing process targets only business-to-business companies. Retail business growth is primarily the traditional territory of the local Chamber of Commerce.

The mission of an economic development corporation is to attract new business into the area, which brings jobs with them. These corporations are one of the key drivers for job growth. As a matter of fact, they take great pride in their ability to attract many new jobs into the area each year. They are also measured on the number of jobs they keep in their geographies as well. So, economic development groups focus both on the attraction and retention issues that surround a geographic area (be it city, town, or village).

Economic development groups are great places for research information, too. They publish many reports on the state of the economy and what companies have moved into an area or are planning to move into the area. Most will also have information on businesses that are either expanding or contracting in your area.

Economic development groups also have networking events that are often open to the public. Get connected to this group and stick with it. In most cases, an online search should enable you to find the economic development organization in your area. In most cases around the country, they are either county-focused or regionally-focused (with several counties included). Either way, this is the place where you will meet the real drivers of business and job growth in your area.

Social Gatherings are Networking Events, Too!

Any social gathering is an opportunity to let people know that you are seeking employment and welcome any assistance they might be able to provide. Your primary goal should be to find out if anyone at your social event might be able to help you directly in your job search. Work a social gathering (birthday party, wedding, barbecue, etc.) similar to the way you would work a business networking event.

Here are a few guidelines to make any social event both enjoyable and productive:

1. Work the room to ensure you meet everyone you can. Find out what they do, let them know what you do, and inform them that you are looking for resources and contacts for your job search.

2. Always be sure you have a supply of business cards on hand and make sure any new contacts you meet have one. Ask them if they have a business card you can have as well.

3. Keep it light but be sure you clearly understand what everyone does for a living and that everyone knows you are looking for assistance in your job search.

4. Follow up with all new contacts. Find ways to help them if you can.

For a long time I never would consider networking at a social event. Time and experience has taught me that you never know who you are going to meet who might be able to help you in some way. Almost any social event I attend these days is an opportunity to meet someone I can do business with. Yes, it is a social event but do not lose sight of your job search campaign either.

Business Meetings

If you are looking for your next position but are still gainfully employed, make sure you treat every business event as an opportunity to network. Be sure you exchange cards and/or information with everyone you meet from your current firm. If you are attending a seminar outside of work, make certain you work the room like any other networking event. Collect and exchange as many business cards as you can. Add them immediately to your contact management system.

Career Fairs

Attending a career fair is about as traditional as you can get in the job search world. Companies come to these events to pitch themselves to job seekers and to build their databases of potential candidates. The company representatives only have so much time during the day to speak with any one individual, so job fairs are a tough environment for trying to sell your self. Sometimes the sheer volume of candidates will often overwhelm the career fair and you will be lucky to talk to someone at all. This is not something I recommend you do.

To get the most out of a job fair with a minimal amount of time invested, do not stand in lines waiting for your one minute opportunity to talk to someone from the firm. Instead, grab as many business cards as you can as you pass by the various employers and vendors. Your goal is to get new contact information that you can add to your networking group. Unless you are at the fair to meet with someone specifically at one of your target employers, your mission is to garner as much information as you can. After you return from the career fair, get that information into your CMS and start networking with these people.

Job fairs are great places to meet people that you can add to your job search network. Outside of that, do not expect too much in the way of a direct job offer while at the fair. Use these fairs as an opportunity to establish some additional contacts for your database and get out.

Alumni Events

Another great way to expand your job search network is by linking back to your college alumni. Many colleges today have active alumni associations that offer opportunities to network both online and offline. While using your alumni status during a job search may seem obvious, you would be surprised at just how few people actually do anything constructive within their alumni associations. Your college alumnus is a very powerful group for you to leverage. By now, all of the people within this group have well-established careers and can help in providing contacts and job leads in your effort expand your job search.

It is well worth creating a separate group within your CMS for alumni contacts. You will probably find many of your college chums already on Facebook or LinkedIn.

Here are a few guidelines for networking within alumni associations:

1. Cast a wide net. Expand your reach beyond that small group of friends you had during college. Consider your entire college alumni association as an open opportunity to add key contacts to your job search network.

2. Focus your initial networking efforts on those in your graduating class and work your way out from there.

3. Be sure you are clear about your intentions. What is it that you want from these potential contacts when you do connect? It should be 1) any direct help they can provide for job leads and 2) any additional contacts they may be willing to share with you that might be helpful in your search. Be clear about what industry and kinds of positions you are seeking.

4. Find ways to help your alumni at the same time. One way networking where you take but do not give back is a dead end. There are plenty who play that game in networking, but in the long run they lose. Nobody likes users and most people can smell them out eventually. Find out if there is anything you can do to help them.

Chapter 9
The Face of Networking: Web 2.0+

No job search campaign would be worth much if it did not combine the best of traditional networking with the Web 2.0+. I emphasize the "+" because the Web itself is constantly changing. There are so many Web sites that are dedicated to networking that your head spins just trying to keep up. Therein lies the only challenge to any web 2.0+ job search strategy: which Web sites should you spend time on?

There are a few networking sites, some of which you may already be signed up for, that are excellent and large enough to make an investment of time worthwhile. Sites such as LinkedIn, Facebook, Ning, PartnerUp, and many others are good places to start if you have not already signed up. All are available to you for free, so you cannot say that it is the money holding you back from starting your online networking.

If you are conducting your job search on a full time basis, then you will have more time to invest in networking sites than those who are holding down a full time job. Nonetheless, there are few points of view on the subject of Web-based networking that are worth noting.

1. You cannot afford not to be utilizing Web-based networking sites for your job search. You will never find a more effective way to find people who can be very helpful in providing key contacts, job leads, and more. If you are not computer literate, then invest in a good course that will help you go from computer illiterate to computer geek. If you do not invest the time to learn your computer well now, you will lose out on the ability to research and meet key contacts while your job competition eats your lunch.

2. Go upscale and have a completely professional-looking profile on any of your networks. I strongly suggest getting a series of professional business photos that you can use for all your profiles. Keep your profile clean and respectable. That does not mean you cannot be social, it just means you have to treat your networking profiles with professional respect regardless of whatever line of business you are in. Dress, act, and look your best. You just never know who is looking at you.

3. Use the scale of mega networking sites to your advantage. To a great extent, networking is a numbers game. The more network contacts you have, the more effective you will be in turning up opportunities in either new contacts and/or job leads. LinkedIn and Facebook are examples of mega sites that have millions of contacts on them from all over the world. The size and scale of these sites allows you to find a richer and more targeted group of potential contacts in your job search.

4. Less is more. Do not sign up for every networking site that comes your way. Stick to two or three at most and work them consistently and regularly. Given the wide array of Web 2.0+ options these days, you can easily find yourself spreading yourself very thin in a short period of time.

5. Think of Web 2.0+ sites as a communication tool for you. You will be able to communicate anything related to your job search including your background, accomplishments, associations, new projects, and other key items to your expanding network base.

6. Make a commitment to invest time each week to maintaining and updating your network profiles. While there are a lot of people getting profiles on Facebook or LinkedIn, many do not know what to do with their profiles after they establish them. Stay focused on meeting new contacts and staying in communication with your network on a regular basis.

Communicating within your network is easy enough to do. For example, Facebook has a feature called What's On Your Mind? that gives you a place to post your latest updates on your job search, share new industry information, or ask your network a question. It is a simple but powerful way to keep your messaging fresh and always in front of your network contacts. LinkedIn has a similar tool as do many networking sites these days.

7. Scan your web 2.0+ contacts for potential contacts you can add to your network. In LinkedIn you can look at the contact group of one of your connections and get an introduction. That is what makes Web 2.0+ networking so effective and efficient at the same time. You are able to locate other contacts and invite them to join your group and network with you.

8. Promote your profiles in every way that you can. Be sure your e-mail signature has the links to your profiles and list the top ones. It does not help to create and manage Web 2.0+ profiles that no one knows about. Do not keep it a secret.

9. Scan trade publications and other media for your industry for key contacts you might want to network with. Once you find the names of some of these people, do a search on their names to see if they have established profiles on key networks, such as LinkedIn and Facebook.

Expert Insights with Adam J. Kovitz

Adam J. Kovitz is the CEO, Editor-in-Chief of The National Networker (www.thenationalnetworker.com), a free online magazine that serves as a positively charged "Consumer Reports of Networking". Check out his blog at http://thenationalnetworker.blogspot.com. He can be reached at adam@thenationalnetworker.com.

Dirks: In the context of conducting a job search, why is it important for today's job seeker to leverage networking both online and off?

Kovitz: I look at networking the way one looks at investing. Wisdom (as well as history) dictates that it is best to diversify one's portfolio. The same can be said with networking, for every network is an asset in that: 1) It is something in which you invest in the hope that it will produce a healthy return 2) It is run by an individual (or group of individuals) that, through their own credibility, will add to the bottom line, and 3) It contains a constantly-evolving portfolio of holdings.

Therefore, it makes sense to include a healthy mix of online as well as offline assets in one's networking portfolio. The mix, however, depends upon the nature of the work desired. For example, jobseekers used to national or even international travel might be more inclined to have a heavier mix towards more online avenues.

Dirks: How can networking improve and extend the reach of a personal brand?

Kovitz: Networking, when done effectively, breaks down boundaries and barriers which would normally impede the flow of information. As the flow increases, visibility increases as more people are exposed to your brand as vast distances are covered. That is the good news.

The bad news is that with the dramatic increase in flow, it becomes more imperative for us to have better filtering mechanisms or risk sensory overload (like attempting to get water from a fire hose with a small paper cup). To this end, effective networking means having a strong sense of self and purpose or risk being swept away in a torrent of chaos.
In short, we must work even harder to make ourselves not only known, but to stand out in the vast global crowd. Our personal brand must be razor-sharp and focused so that the proper keywords are found by an ever-savvy, ever-demanding audience.

Dirks: What are the advantages of leveraging social marketing/networking during a job search?

Kovitz: There are several key advantages. 1) Increasing the quantity of those you might know; 2) Increasing the quality of those connections; 3) Increasing the quantity of things you know; and 3) Enhancing the quality of what you know.

Dirks: There are so many Web sites/resources that offer networking opportunities today. How would you suggest a job seeker narrow down their choices of which social networks will be most effective for them (outside of job aggregators like HotJobs, Monster, etc.)?

Kovitz: I find that it helps to network with contacts in your particular field (or target company) and interview them. If that is not an option, find a career transition network, a career coach. Ask the network these questions: 1) What online resources do they use to find qualified candidates? 2) Are there specific resources for specific types of jobs (i.e., Dice.com for IT professionals)? 3) Which organizations do they use for executive/job search?

Dirks: What are five common mistakes you see people make when they try to engage online networking using sites such as Linkedin and Facebook?

Kovitz: Common mistakes include:

1)   approaching such networks without a plan or purpose as to what should be accomplished.

2)   Mixing business with pleasure; the last thing I want to see in a prospective employee are spring break pictures from his college days. Having both LinkedIn and Facebook accounts, I tend to use LinkedIn strictly for my professional life while Facebook is more personal.

3)   Coming off as too eager to sell their product, service, or themselves. One does not propose marriage on a first date.

4)   Connecting with just anyone. If you want to be perceived as great, surround yourself with great people. I have a strong aversion to linking with or "friending" multilevel marketers or other "get rich quick" folks, unless I have already have an offline relationship with them.

5)   Over-diversifying. There is the tendency to try every social network there is to try. We have the same twenty-four hours a day as everyone else and the investment in networking is of your time, energy, and effort. Choose carefully.

Some Web 2.0+ Options

Even though there are a great many Web options available for networking, for the purposes of this book, we will sample just a few. LinkedIn and Facebook represent two fine examples of Web-based networking platforms that should be seriously considered by anyone conducting a job search campaign.

Facebook

What started out as a great software program for networking college students has turned into one of the largest Web-centric networks in the world. Over the past few years, Facebook has managed to attract and retain a wider range of ages. You are just as likely to find your business colleagues on Facebook as much as you are your teenage son or daughter.

Do not be fooled by the social aspects of Facebook. Facebook is a powerful business networking tool and provides the job seeker with an array of tools that cannot be beat. Employers and recruiters alike have established profiles on Facebook that enable them to interact with potential job seekers like never before. It is networking sites like Facebook that have made job aggregators like Monster or HotJobs look old school in comparison.

With millions of active users on Facebook, the potential to reach employers and job candidates on the site is vast. Facebook provides a variety of tools, from applications to pages and groups, which, when combined with the power of your social graph, make networking, job hunting, and finding the perfect candidate easier than ever.

Top Ten Tips for Job Searching on Facebook
(Presented here courtesy of Facebook.com)

1. The Professional Profile: Start with the basics by highlighting your skills and experience on your profile. Complete the education and work section, and use the description portion to highlight responsibilities, skills, and accomplishments. Remember to provide work-appropriate contact information, and leave e-mail addresses such as likesagoodparty@gmail.com off your profile.

Go the extra mile and install the Professional Profile application (http://tinyurl.com/6u6f8f), which turn your social connections into business connections by consolidating professional information into a tab on your profile.

2. Use Friend Lists for Work Lists: Create Friend Lists to group together your employment and networking contacts. Specify in profile privacy settings and album privacy settings what each Friend List can and cannot view. Keep the party pictures from last weekend for your friends, and the more appropriate pictures accessible to your work contacts.

3. Network in an industry group: Join an industry-focused Facebook group pertinent to your field to network with new people and stay active in discussions on the Group Wall. For instance, The Ad Group (http://tinyurl.com/7orowu) has more than 8,000 members, and allows advertising professionals to meet and share information about their industry.

4. Keep things private: Utilize Facebook's profile privacy settings to control who can see your profile, and make a good impression by understanding the settings and projecting an appropriate image. Start by determining who can view your profile by selecting access for networks, friends of friends, or just friends. From there, determine what those people can and cannot see on your profile, such as status updates, tagged photos, personal information, friends, and wall posts.

5. Leverage your social graph: Just as you would in the offline world, use Facebook to spread the word that you are looking for a job. Reach out to friends for help in your search to find out if they know of openings or relevant contacts. Drop a note to friends in your industry to alert them that you are looking for your next career move, and become Facebook friends with people who you have met socially to get the networking ball rolling. And what better way to reach everyone than with your status update? Specify what you are seeking for widest reach.

6. Find and make college contacts: Find your college alumni association's Facebook Page to stay in contact with former classmates who might work in your field. Oftentimes, specific schools within the university also have pages for alumni to interact with each other and post information.

7. Utilize CareerBuilder on Facebook: Tap into one of the largest online job sites with CareerBuilder's Facebook Page (www.facebook. com/careerbuilder), complete with a variety of employers looking for candidates. CareerBuilder also offers a range of sub-pages for several specific categories such as healthcare, IT, sales and marketing, and engineering. Become a "fan" to monitor job listings, companies hiring, and to apply for open positions.

8. Sky's the limit for employers: Facebook offers a multitude of opportunities for employers to attract the right pool of potential hires, including developing interactive applications (such as J.P. Morgan, http://apps.facebook.com/jpmorgancommunity/) and Facebook Pages to keep "fans" updated. Many employers also participate in job

search Pages, such as CareerBuilder's, where they can interact directly with Facebook users. Job hunters can take advantage of employers on Facebook by ensuring that they have developed a competitive and intelligent presence on the site as well.

9. Interact with friends and employers: During the job seeking process, you can also install career-oriented Facebook applications and have updates sent directly to your profile.

10. Find the companies recruiting on Facebook: Seek out specific companies that have created Facebook pages to recruit employees and regularly post openings, videos, events, and company information. "Fan" the pages and monitor listings to learn more about what type of employees they are looking for.

Examples include:
- Ernst & Young: http://www.facebook.com/ernstandyoungcareers?ref=s
- Microsoft: http://tinyurl.com/8ja3eq
- General Electric: http://tinyurl.com/75x2cm
- U.S. Customs and Border Patrol: http://tinyurl.com/7r8wu8
- Aerotek: http://tinyurl.com/9ygjv4

Search for additional pages here: http://www.facebook.com/pages/?browse, and use search terms such as recruiting, your industry, or company names to narrow your search.

LinkedIn

From a purely business point of view, there are few networking sites that can compare to the networking power of LinkedIn. This is not a social networking site; this is a full-scale business networking site that every job searcher needs to be on, regardless of what industry or business you are in. Unlike Facebook, which offers a more relaxed way to network, LinkedIn is all business. The look, feel, and networking power give LinkedIn all the right options for any job searcher.

Here are some ways to ensure you leverage LinkedIn to harness its full networking potential during your job search:

1. Have a complete LinkedIn profile. According to LinkedIn, users with complete profiles are forty times more likely to receive opportunities through LinkedIn than users with incomplete profiles. If you want to improve your ability to be picked up by search engines like Google, having a complete profile will help improve your search engine optimization (SEO). Include all of the e-mails that you use so LinkedIn users can contact you easily.

Add a professional-looking photo of yourself. Add a profile summary that helps other users learn what you do. This is a great place to showcase your skills and knowledge. Provide a complete and accurate employment and education history. If you have a blog and a personal Web site, make sure these are listed as well. In short, make sure you provide information for every nook and cranny within your LinkedIn profile.

2. This is all about your personal branding. LinkedIn, like any other networking platform, is a place you can showcase your personal brand. The place to showcase your brand is in the summary section of your profile. Have a clear brand message that tells the story of what you stand for professionally. Be descriptive but concise. What value do you deliver? What are you really about? What message do you have for someone looking at your profile? Be compelling and clear about who and what you are about. Your personal brand reputation is at stake.

3. In the education section of LinkedIn, you will have an opportunity to list all your schools, majors, and activities both in and out of the classroom. This section should be as detailed as possible.

4. Set your profile so that your entire profile can be viewed by other users. In a job search campaign, this is your opportunity to give anyone who happens to see your profile an opportunity to fully explore it. A full and fully viewable profile works for your on a 24/7 basis.

5. LinkedIn makes it easy for you to start building your base by enabling you to upload contacts from your current e-mail lists. Of course, you can add your contacts manually as well. Using LinkedIn's address book importer you can invite your contacts to join LinkedIn and accept your offer to connect with them.

To improve your results in the number of people who respond positively to your invitation, send them a personalized message from you via LinkedIn. Spend the extra few seconds it takes to add their first names and any other personal comments.

Here is the standard LinkedIn message that you will find on an invitation to connect:

I'd like to add you to my professional network on LinkedIn.
- David

That kind of message is okay but not really compelling. By adding just a bit of personalization, you will find that you will convert more invitations to connect into new contacts for your network base.

Try something like this instead:

Mike:
I hope this e-mail finds you and your family well! It has been a few years but I would like to add you to my professional network on LinkedIn and reconnect.
- David Dirks

Just a bit of personalization can help to send the message home that you spent the time to add a personal touch to a usually benign message.

6. Get three or more recommendations from your network of contacts. Past managers you have worked for and colleagues who have worked with you directly are each opportunities for getting a

recommendation. LinkedIn makes it easy for you to ask someone for a recommendation. Be sure that when you make your request, you ask the person if he can specifically make a "strong and positive" recommendation on your behalf. Even though you have the ability to accept, reject, or have the person revise a recommendation, it is best to make sure the person is willing to give you the strongest and most positive recommendation he can.

7. Monitor the question and answer section. This section of your LinkedIn profile allows you to selectively answer questions from other LinkedIn users. This is an opportunity for you to showcase your expertise and really help someone else in the process. Always add your links (e-mail, blog, personal Web site) to any answer you give in this section.

8. Put your own questions out into the LinkedIn network using the LinkedIn Answers function. What challenges are going on in your industry? You can ask any relevant business question but also try to pose questions around what job search strategies and tactics are showing results (for those also in a job search). You have the power to find out what others are thinking, so harness this LinkedIn feature and make it work on your behalf.

9. Join other networking groups. LinkedIn offers thousands of groups and you can find more than a few that are built around your interests. Use the search directory to find out what groups are available. Check them out and join the ones that seem active and appropriate for your job search interests. You will also notice groups that others in your network have joined, so check those out, too. Once you have joined a group, you will be able to find and contact other members of the group. This is a very powerful and efficient way to grow your network base.

10. Search previous employers and find contacts that you know and reconnect with them. This is a pretty quick way to build your base of network contacts during your job search.

11. Be sure you contact people that you know or people you can get introduced to. LinkedIn is pretty sensitive about people who just try to throw every contact they find into their network. Stick to who you know so you do not get your privileges blocked by LinkedIn.

12. LinkedIn offers you a place to basically post your updated résumé. Be as descriptive as possible and use keywords that people looking for your type of experience will recognize and understand.

13. Take advantage of the LinkedIn Jobs search engine. Typically, there are thousands of listings. Search using keywords, company, location, or title to find job leads you can use during your campaign.

The JobsInsider function allows you to see who within your LinkedIn network that work at a specific hiring company. When you open any job posting at CareerBuilder, SimplyHired, Dice, HotJobs, Indeed, Monster, Craigslist, or Vault, JobsInsider will help you locate someone within your network who could help you with an introduction to the hiring manager for that job. It is another powerful tool to make your job search networking both effective and efficient.

14. Use and update the "What are you doing" sections of LinkedIn (and all other network platforms that offer it) as often as possible. Let people know what you are working on or looking for. This is an often overlooked feature that can really help keep you in front of others in your network. Any updates you make to this section are automatically noted on the home pages of your LinkedIn network members.

15. It is not about who you know; it is about who they know. Always remember that your network contacts know people. It is your job to comb through your network to find other potential contacts that could prove helpful during a job search.

16. Share your knowledge and expertise. Your goal is to establish yourself as an expert in your field. The only way to get that is to make sure you participate in LinkedIn both with individual contacts and

groups. Over time, you will gain a ton of credibility with the people you network with by sharing your expertise, insights, and time to help others. You might even learn a thing or two along the way!

17. Make a face-to-face or phone call meeting your goal. Never make the mistake of running your Web 2.0+ job search with the notion that you never have to see anyone or speak to anyone on the phone. It might seem old school, but face-to-face interactions and phone calls are the cement of strong business relationships.

Ning: Creating Your Own Social Network

Ning (www.Ning.com) is another Web 2.0+ creation that makes it easy for you to extend your personal brand and networking via your own networking site that can be hosted for free. Think about this: You have the power to create your own social networking site around your expertise, industry, etc. Using the power of your network of connections, you will have the ability to supply your social network with a steady stream of people who share the same interests.

By itself, creating a social network via a platform like Ning will not single-handedly solve your job search problem. However, it will go a long way to giving you the opportunity to share ideas, expand your personal brand, and establish additional contacts for job search networking. As your social network grows, so grows your ability to create new contacts. It is a beautiful thing.

Using Ning to Expand Your Social Networking Base

Information courtesy of: Ning, Inc. (www.Ning.com).
Used with permission. All rights reserved.

Ning's flagship application is your own social network for anything. Launched in February 2007, your own social network for anything gives individuals and companies the ability to rapidly create and scale entirely new social networks. Your own social network for anything offers over fifty different visual themes as well as the option to completely control the administration of a social network. The application offers a wide choice of features—videos, photos, chat, music, groups, events, and blogs—in addition to a latest activity stream, member profile pages, friends, messaging, e-mail notifications, RSS support, and third party applications a member or Ning Creator chooses to add to their social network on Ning. As a result of this broad set of choices, each social network on Ning is unique and special in its purpose, design, branding, and features.

Ning Creators can choose to moderate members before they join or simply show the social network's homepage to non-members. Members of social networks have full control over who sees their profiles and content within a social network or on Ning.com.

Ning was started with a simple premise: When people have the freedom to create a new social experience online, uniquely customized for the most important people and interests in their lives with no effort, no cost, and infinite choice, the world is a better, more colorful and certainly more interesting place in which to live.

With Ning, people are creating new social experiences that are:
* Infinitely customizable
* Beautifully designed
* Easily created and moderated

Ning and networking platforms similar to it are a great way to create the differentiation you need in any job market to separate you from the crowd. While it takes some investment on your part, the rewards of promoting your own specialized social network in the context of your job search campaign can be a powerful accelerator of success. It is all about finding the career opportunities you want!

Here are some examples of specialized social networking sites created using Ning:

http://mrspace.ning.com for market researchers
http://jobertalk.ning.com

I created my own networking site, http://jobsearchmarketing. ning.com based on this book. If you are in a job search, I highly encourage you to become a member to help you expand your job search and its ultimate success! Help me to make it the largest job search networking site around!

Microblogging: Twitter

First we were introduced to blogging; now we have microblogging. Tomorrow, who knows what the latest trend will be? Mircroblogging aims to satisfy those who thirst for communication on a 24/7 basis. Microblogging services, such as Twitter, give you the opportunity to send and receive messages to and from just about any computing/communications platform. Twitter is the largest and most known of the microblogging services.

There is a lot of very useful content on Twitter that makes this platform ideal for someone in the job search campaign mode. The key to using the Web is being able to create filters that allow you to sift out the junk and focus on the meaty pieces that are applicable to your job search efforts. Think of microblogs as just another way to communicate and network.

Let's take a look at some constructive ways to use microblogging platforms:

1. Use Twitter to connect and network with people in your industry. Using the Twitter search function, you can search for people or by topic.

2. Link Twitter to your other social networking sites. For example, you can link your Twitter account with your Facebook account so that your "tweets," or messages, show up on your Facebook profile.

3. It is a great way to find out the latest on job search strategies and tactics. Twitter is a treasure trove of content, links, resources, and ideas.

4. From a personal branding point of view, Twitter offers a great way to expand the reach of your blogs, podcasts, and personal Web sites. If you are working to position yourself as a thought leader within your area of expertise and/or industry, Twitter is another way reinforce that positioning. Simply post a tweet on your latest blog topic and be sure you add the link so people can find your blog.

If you want to see how people are using Twitter to advance their causes and establish themselves as "thought leaders" in their field, just search the key words that best describes your industry.

For example, if you type in the word "marketing" into the Twitter search field you will find several people who had offer marketing advice in the form of tweets. I found a Twitter site called ideas4rent, which had over 20,000 followers who subscribed to tweets on his ideas on growing a business. On the Twitter site he has links back to his Web site. Some people choose to link their latest blog postings on a tweet, which helps them drive traffic back to the blog.

5. During your job search, you can set up a feed for receiving information on potential job leads. For example, you can create searches on job opportunities. Let's say you are searching for jobs in the automotive industry. Within a few seconds you will find the Twitter site, fish4autojobs. Click on the site to find lots of tweets on a wide variety of automotive related jobs. Or let's say you are looking for job leads in the computer programming field. Using the advanced search function, type in "computer jobs" in the All of These Words search box. The result is pages of tweets that are related to computer jobs posted from all over the country.

You could narrow the search even more by creating a geographic parameter in the advanced search area. In the "places" section within

Twitter's advanced search area, you can input the city or town and state you live in and tell the search you want to look no further than X miles from that point for tweets related to computer jobs.

Once you find the job search tweets that you think are helpful, you can subscribe to these tweets. Once you subscribe to a particular tweet, you will see those updated tweets from your subscribed listed on your Twitter homepage. You can easily unsubscribe if you find that the tweets are not what you need or want.

The advanced search function on Twitter gives you the ability to search the vast depth of tweets and cut through the clutter to find what you need to advance your job search. That is the key to microblogging: find the right people with the right topics that can help you sniff out job leads and other opportunities. They are in there. You just have dig them out and sift through to find the tweets and people that are going to add value to your job search efforts.

6. Get a custom Twitter background. If you are going to do Twitter in any serious way, a good investment is some design work around your profile page that works in concert with your personal branding. It is not a bad idea to create a simple knock-off from your personal Web site and/or blog site so you have some brand continuity. You can create a Twitter background for free at sites like www.twitbacks.com; www.Twitterbacks.com; www.mytweetspace.com; and www.freeTwitterdesigner.com. Alternately, sites such as www.Twitterimage.com can really beef up your professional appearance for a small fee.

7. Use a professional picture. Preferably, you should be using the same picture on all of your social and business networking sites. You want people to be able to recognize you over time, so using different photos or having no photo at all is not helpful.

8. Add and register your Twitter profile into the yellow pages of Twitter, such as sites like twellow.com. This is a directory of Twitter profiles and helps people who are searching for specific types of expertise

or people. You can greatly expand your profile to include more information. Sites like www.twellow.com are another way to extend your personal brand and reach.

9. Ask questions in your tweets to get some dialogue going on Twitter. Whether it is about a pressing industry issue or a great business book you have just read, create a way to interact with others on Twitter.

10. Set up a specific schedule for using Twitter during the day. There is no need to Twitter all the time. Like everything else, you have to pace yourself and establish a rhythm that works best for you. Spend time doing three things on Twitter: 1) expanding your thought leadership position with ideas, questions, and thoughts related to your expertise; 2) using the advanced search function to find sources for job leads and other opportunities; and 3) use Twitter as a way to link people to your other resources, such as your professional blog, Web site, podcasts, etc.

11. Do a Web search to find "Twitter tools" that can help you become more effective and efficient with microblogging sites. Conduct this kind of search often as there are new tools appearing online almost every day.

Microblogging does have a place within a job search campaign. How you decide to use it will determine if you spend more time doing busy work or more time finding new networking contacts and job leads.

Google Profile

Google offers you the opportunity to give your personal branding a broader reach with the Google profile. It takes only a few minutes to put together a Google profile, and such a profile setup allows you to add a personal photo, short bio, education history, some personal info, and, most importantly, your key Web links.

Here is what mine looks like:

www.google.com/profiles/dirksmarketing

According to Google's Web site, "A Google profile is simply how you present yourself on Google products to other Google users. It allows you to control how you appear on Google and tells others a bit more about who you are. With a Google profile, you can easily share your Web content on one central location. You can include, for example, links to your blog, online photos, and other profiles such as Facebook, LinkedIn, and more. You have control over what others see. Your profile will not display any private information unless you have explicitly added it.

"You can also allow people to find you more easily by enabling your profile to be searched by your name. Simply set your existing profile to show your full name publicly.

"If you have been writing reviews on Google Maps, creating articles on Google Knol, sharing Google Reader items, or adding books to your Google Book Search library, you may already have a profile."

Passive Web 2.0 Strategies

There was a time not long ago when large job aggregators such as HotJobs, Monster, CareerBuilder, Indeed, and others were the places to be if you wanted to find a job.

You simply post your résumé, set your job finders to match the parameters of the jobs you are looking for, and sit back and wait for things to come to you. Is this effective? In a great job market where there is a shortage of qualified employees, yes. In a depressed job market, not so much.

So the only question we need to answer is this: What role does passive job search play within your job search campaign? The answer is that passive online strategies still have an important role to play in your job search. My approach to a job search campaign is that you should leave no stone unturned. Put every possible resource to work and focus the bulk of your time and energy on those resources that have the most promise for developing job leads. The only difference today is that these passive online strategies do not play a central role like they used to before Web sites such as LinkedIn showed up.

Here is my list of ways to maximize the effectiveness of passive job aggregators.

1. Set your expectations low. Job boards and aggregators are mass marketing machines in the job search world. Yes, they are large, but this fact can sometimes work against them. Aggregators and job boards are often filled with "junk jobs" that sound like real jobs but are really multilevel marketing (MLM) schemes. Many of the jobs posted on these sites are through recruiters and not direct company-placed jobs. Going through a recruiter is not necessarily a bad thing, but connecting with the company directly cuts down on the clutter and cycle time it takes to get connected with a real hiring manager. It also seems that more and more retained and in-house recruiters are moving to places such as LinkedIn, Facebook, and more targeted on- and offline networking platforms to find the right candidates. So, do not expect a whole lot of action here, and invest your time accordingly. I recommend spending less time with job boards and more time checking companies that post their active positions on their Web sites.

2. Set it and forget it (or at least check in with less frequency). Set the job search engine within each job board/aggregator so that the site can contact you if it finds the jobs that match your requirements. Check on the postings as they come into your e-mail but do not spend a lot of time here. Set it, check it, and get out.

3. Narrow your searches down as much as possible. Be as specific as you can to what the job titles are and the geographic area you are willing to work in. If you are too broad on either job definition or geography, your e-mail box will be crammed with junk.

4. Use job boards as a research tool. This is particularly helpful in the early stages of your job search. Use the search functions on these sites to see what the range of positions are posted within your geographic area. Start out with a broad search first. For example, if you wanted to see anything related to marketing, you'd enter the word "marketing" into the search function. Progressively, keep narrowing your key words by making them more specific. So, instead of marketing, you might try "marketing director" first and see how much of the clutter (i.e., jobs that are not even remotely what you are looking for) is reduced.

5. Keep your information updated. It is easy to forget you even have an account on some job boards over time.

6. Job boards/aggregators are great sources of information on the job search process. You will find volumes of articles, podcasts, and white papers (the business equivalent to a college research paper) that can sometimes be helpful during a job search. These sites provide great information on tooling your résumé, preparing for a job interview, and all other things that only come after you have been able to find the job opportunity.

7. Do not spend any money on upgrades or premium services unless you feel absolutely compelled to do so. I recommend using the free services offered and leave it at that.

Leaving No Stone Unturned

In a job search campaign, leaving no stone unturned means taking advantage of any tool, online or off, that could help you generate job leads. Some networking opportunities are going to be more effective and productive for you than others. As you develop and implement your job search plan, keep this in mind everyday. Reduce time spent on job search tools and platforms that are good to have but are not worth a large portion of your available time.

The combination of both face-to-face and online networking resources and platforms is the best way to ensure you are getting the best return for the time you invest in networking. There is no one way to do things during a job search campaign. You will be better served if you tailor your job search to utilize those networking resources that are best suited to your personality and experience.

That said, you will also need to push yourself to develop competencies in areas that you normally try to avoid. For example, if you feel uncomfortable in business networking situations, consider that practice makes perfect and the only way to get better is to just start doing it. In this example, you might want to tag along with a friend who is an effective networker and skilled in the art of meeting and engaging people he has never met before.

Networking is not for everyone, but everyone who wants to generate job leads needs to seriously consider some level of networking in order to be successful and find the right job opportunities.

Chapter 10
Becoming a Research Powerhouse

If I had to rate the essential skills you need in order to generate the kinds of job leads that will bring employment success, research skills would rate among the top of the list (networking, both traditional and Web 2.0+ rate the highest). Your ability to utilize both traditional (i.e., resources you would find in your local library) as well as Web 2.0+ (i.e., Google) resources is in direct correlation to your success in finding and generating job opportunities during your job search campaign.

You need to be able to identify resources and use them to your advantage to find:

- The key decision makers for any particular position your may be targeting. Key decision makers are those who have the ability to make a direct hiring decision.
- New networking contacts within your area of interest and/ or career expertise
- Job opportunity leads (i.e., via company job boards, if they have them)
- Companies that are healthy and hiring
- Associations and other organizations within your career field that could be a resource for job leads or networking connections
- The key industry issues and areas that are hot topics within your field of expertise
- New growth sectors within your field that could provide potential job opportunities

During a job search, you have to become a skilled researcher, someone who can locate information on demand that can be leveraged for the job search. Like the ability to network effectively with people, your ability to conduct job research will be critical to the outcome of your goal to find job opportunities you can apply yourself to.

Tips on Becoming a Research Powerhouse

1. Frame any research you do during the course of your job search in the form of a question to save you time and make you more effective. Spend your research time answering specific questions related to your job search rather than some general non-question research pursuit. For example, "What companies are likely to be hiring green energy experts?"

2. Take advantage of all research sources including broadcast news, newspapers, popular magazines, journals, books, government publications, Internet, shareholder annual reports, and reference materials. It is generally not a good idea to rely on just one or two sources. The key is to have a narrowly-defined question but leverage a wide array of research resources to answer your question(s).

3. Ask for help. Do not go it alone when you can easily make a phone call to the local library to ask for help. Asking for help can also be accomplished by using your network of business and personal contacts. LinkedIn, for example, offers you a way to ask a question of your network contact list and/or any special group you belong to within LinkedIn. You will save yourself a lot of time and effort by utilizing both your library resources and your network.

4. Stay organized. Any job search campaign worth its salt will require some consistent level of investigation and research. There will always be some new information popping up along the campaign trail that will require you to invest some time in getting more details. Whether you are searching for an individual, group, or corporation, you will need to make sure you have a way to organize your information.

There is nothing quite like the feeling you get when you cannot find some vital information you just found. Losing information you need in order to win the job search game will have you wondering if you have lost your marbles.

Get organized and stay organized.

Traditional Research Opportunities

Your Local Library

Once thought to be a dinosaur that was about to crash because of the introduction of the Internet, your local library remains a vibrant and powerful ally in your job search campaign. Most municipalities have access to a library, whether it is a local library or college/university library.

Here is a general walk-through tour of your typical local library reference section.

Web Access: If you do not have access to a PC at home, then you will find computers available at your local library. There is no excuse for not utilizing the Internet for a job search. If you have a library, chances are you will have access to the Internet as well.

The Reference Section: Here you will find the bulk of resources that can aid you during your job search campaign. We will cover a select group in this section but can by no means cover them all.

The smartest move you can make at your local library is to get very familiar with what resources the library offers. Go to the librarian for a tour of the resources available, from Internet to hardcopy reference materials.

Let the librarian know you are in a job search and have him show you some of the more appropriate reference materials that would be helpful during your search. The librarian will be very happy to help you, and this help will reduce your learning curve. Do not assume you know all of the resources that your library has to offer.

Not all reference resources will be in every library. If you do not see a specific reference title noted in this book, ask the librarian if there is another substitute for it.

American Library Association Guide to Information Access
Publisher: Random House

To bone up on your research skills, this reference book provides an overview of 3,000+ standard and electronic sources in many of the most researched subject categories. It will tell you where to find these sources and explains the latest research methods.
For extra information on your job search, check out the "Business and Finance," "Jobs and Careers," and "Small Business" sections of the book.

Business Information Resources, 3rd Edition
Publisher: University of California Press

Besides being a great way to learn the basic and advanced researching skills, this reference book covers an immense amount of business information resources. If you need resources for energy industry statistics, for example, this book can help you find them. The book covers a wide range of business information resources ranging from accounting, taxation, general management, computers and MIS (management information systems), corporate finance/banking, insurance, real estate, international management, human resources, production, and operations management. Dig in and find out what you can use for your job search. Sections of particular interest to job search include "Industry Statistics" and "Locating Information on Companies, Organizations, and Individuals."

Encyclopedia of Associations
Publisher: Thomson Gale

Associations are great places to find additional job resources, and associations present a huge opportunity to network within your industry or area of expertise. This book comes in several large volumes and lists association contact information, such as address, phone, e-mail, Web site, key contact person, and a short blurb about the association.

Use the "keyword list" to find the appropriate associations that are targeted for your industry or area of career interest. For example, the keyword "aerospace" has seven sections that are applicable to that keyword. Using keywords is a very effective and efficient way to find what you need in this encyclopedia.

State and Regional Associations of the United States
National Trade and Professionals Associations of the United States 2009
Publisher: Columbia Books, Inc.

This directory lists 8,000 trade associations, professional societies, labor unions, and other similar groups on a state or regional level. This is probably a good place to start searching for those associations that can lead to networking opportunities. For example, a graphic designer living in New York State might be interested in checking out the New York Chapter of the American Institute of Graphic Art, or the Association of Graphic Communications, or perhaps the Graphic Artists Guild of New York. Many of these organizations have regular networking opportunities during the year.

The *National Trade and Professional Associations 2009* directory is much larger and will take a bit more time to peruse, but it probably has several associations you can target for networking and other job search information.

In both books, each lists the key contact person for the organization. Call the contact person to find out what the organization might suggest you do in light of your job search for networking contacts and developing job opportunity leads.

Gale Directory of Publications and Broadcast Media
Publisher: Thomson Gale

This book identifies the media outlets that you can send press releases to and also offers freelance writing opportunities, or a source for expert industry information. This is a state-by-state listing that allows you to narrow your media research down to the villages, towns, and cities that are within your search.

Reference Guides for Geographies

If you are evaluating a geographical move in search of job opportunities and/or are conducting research on the types of industries and companies located within specific areas, then the following reference tools are for you.

America's Top Rated Cities: A Statistical Handbook
Publisher: Grey House Publishing

This is an excellent resource tool for getting both business and living environment information on a wide range of cities across the United States. This book provides an overview of the local economy, income, and businesses located or headquartered in each region, among other things. For example, if you are researching Durham, North Carolina, you could find out where most people are employed and the occupations with the greatest projected employment growth for Durham in a specified period of time. This book also gives you specific details on average wages by occupation. For most cities, you will find a listing of major employers, which is key if you are targeting specific companies in specific industries.

For those who live or want to live and work in the suburbs, you will find *The Comparative Guide to American Suburbs* by Grey House Publishing a valuable tool for geographic targeting as well.

State Profiles: The Population and Economy of Each U.S. State 3rd Edition
Publisher: Bernan Press

This is another excellent state by state guide; pay particular attention the following sections: "Labor Market," "Economic Activity," and "Exports."

The National Job Bank
Publisher: Adams Media

This book offers great state listings with an alphabetical listing in each state section of employers and summary information that includes contact information and a description of employers and the types of positions they typically advertise and seek. For target company research, this is a good place to start.

The Directory of Executive Recruiters
Publisher: Kennedy Information

This reference book contains information on 16,000+ recruiters. It breaks down the recruitment industry into eighty-four management functions and 121 industries, which makes it easier for you to find the recruitment firms that are best suited for the types of career opportunities you need and want. The book contains excellent tips on how to best utilize recruitment firms, as well.

Vocational Careers Sourcebook

While this is basically a career planning reference tool, the book does contain some excellent and useful information for job searchers. It covers a very wide range of occupations and careers.

Sections for the job searcher to focus on include "Associations" (networking contacts and other resources), "Periodicals" (specifically related to that occupation/career), and "Meetings & Conventions" (potential places to network).

The Corporate Directory
Publisher: Walker's Research

This expansive directory has excellent summary information on over 10,000 publicly held United States Corporations. It has financial, management, and stock data in broad company profiles.

Headquarters USA 2009
Publisher: Omnigraphics, Inc.

This reference book lists over 114,000+ headquarters (and other central offices) for some of the largest and most important corporations, organizations, agencies, and institutions in the United States. If you need to find the address, phone, and fax number for a corporation, you will probably find it here.

Small Business Sourcebook
Publisher: Thomson Gale

This reference book has two valuable purposes. 1) If you are interested in starting your own business, you will find a treasure trove of data on places to start your research. 2) For the job seeker, it is an excellent way to get information on any career field and the resources that could help your networking efforts during your job search. Key job search resources, such as trade publications, associations, tradeshows/conventions, and computerized databases are just a few of those listed. Think about the networking opportunities you will find that might lead you to finding job opportunities within your career field.

Job Hunter's Sourcebook
Publisher: Thomson Gale

This is another reference book designed with the job searcher in mind. The book lists, by profession, many great sources of information, such as employer directories, networking lists, online job sources/services, tradeshows, and other resources that can be very helpful during a job search campaign.

2009 Writer's Market
Publisher: Writer's Digest Books

Built specifically for freelance writers, this book is also a great reference tool for job seekers. It uncovers writing opportunities for almost any industry you can think of. Even if you have no ambition to add to your personal brand by writing and publishing articles, the book is an excellent source of information for contacts. For instance, if you were in the women's apparel industry, you would find contact information for the editorial staff of women's fashion magazines.

Having access to a contact's information can be very helpful for the job seeker. For example, the job seeker could contact the editor of the magazine and ask him some questions, such as:

- Does he know of employers in the industry that are hiring?
- Can he help you identify other industry contacts that you could leverage during your job search?
- What other resources, both online and offline, does he recommend you use during your job search?

You can add more questions as you go on but the idea is to use the information presented in these books as your ticket to finding other targeted opportunities to expand your network contacts.

Again, this is not a complete list of reference tools a library has available. Every library is different, and much of your success depends on your ability to learn how to use the library to your advantage. Ask, and you will find it there.

Your local library is not only a great place to conduct your job campaign research, but it is also a place to do some quiet thinking. Your local library has plenty of resources beyond what is covered in this book that can be leveraged during your job search.

Researching Effectively with Google

Online search can provide you with the kinds of information you will need in order to unearth new networking contacts, sources of information, and, ultimately, job leads. However, if not done effectively, online search can suck up valuable hours of time that could be used for more actionable activities.

Google has clearly had a huge impact on the way we think about and conduct online searches. Its relevance to job search is multiplied by the number of variables that can be researched within the context of a search. You can locate people, places, and things that once were unobtainable by using traditional search methods. What used to take days or weeks to research can now take seconds. That is the good news.

The not-so-good news is that Internet search is a deep and wide lake of information. It is called the Worldwide Web for a reason. The challenge using any search engine is that it can produce too much information.

Let's learn how to conduct online searches that get right to the heart of the information needed, and quickly. Here are a few things you should know about the Google search interface and the features that are contained within it.

1. I'm Feeling Lucky tab: Instead of seeing all the results of your search query, Google activates the link and takes you to the first result of the search. It is a very limited function.

2. Advanced Search: It is recommended that you use this page for all of your search queries. Being able to have Google search for just

specific key words and leave out other specific words helps you stay focused.

3. The advanced search features of Google also allow you to search for specific file types (i.e., PDF files versus MS Word documents) as well as specific Web sites. For example, if you want to conduct a search query on "marketing jobs" within just the IBM.com Web site, the Google search engine would crawl through the IBM Web site to find the relevant links.

4. If you want to Google a specific person's name, just type in the name and include a middle initial if you can. The middle initial helps to separate out the contact from the others with the same first and last name. Enter the name into the "this exact wording or phrase" query section, and let the search begin. This is a quick way to pare down the number of results and focus on the exact person. Another way to find a specific person by name is to put quotation marks around the name in the search box.

5. Watch the words you use in your search queries. In Google, every word counts, and so it pays to make sure you use only those words that are relevant to what you need to find. Keep your queries simple, and resist the temptation to add more words to the search query. Simple is better.

6. Avoid using superfluous words. You do not need to use words like in, an, of, the, is and who, etc. Google ignores words like these.

7. Do not ask questions such as, "How many marketing jobs are open in New York State?" might seem targeted but in fact this kind of question query may eliminate useful documents in your search results.

8. Word order counts in your query. Placing key words on the front end of your search tends to make your search more effective. Google will prioritize the word order and search based on that priority and order of words.

9. Asterisks are another way for you to narrow your search results. If you are looking for current jobs in the pharmaceutical field, you would type it as: current*pharmaceutical*jobs. Or, a search for sales management jobs in New York State would be listed as sales*management*jobs*ny. Asterisks are powerful tools to aid you in your search for job leads. Add a date or timeframe to your asterisk search query. For example, sales*management*jobs*ny*2009 will define and narrow your search to jobs that contain the date 2009.

10. Do not bother with punctuation. For the most part, Google ignores it.

11. Use the "tilde" (~) operator. What the tilde operator does is allow you to expand your search to synonyms. For example, open positions ~medical will also give you positions in healthcare, medicine, etc. It is a great way to narrow your search but also allows similar positions to fill the results queue.

12. Narrow your search to within a site or domain by simply adding "sales positions site:www.apple.com" and it will search only within the Apple.com Web site for sales positions and related items.

13. Use the official Google cheat sheet: www.google.com/help/cheatsheet

14. Also reference this Google section: www.google.com/intl/en/help/features
Google search is one of the best things to hit the job search campaign trail. If you remember that your goal is to 1) find direct job leads; 2) discover new resources that may lead you to job leads; and 3) meet new people to connect and network with who may lead you to job leads. Focus and narrow your search around these three goals when using Google search and you will find yourself spending more time reviewing the right search results and not having to weed out junk.

Paul Krupin on Search
www.magicsearching.com

One of the biggest problems people encounter in the job search is using too few words in Internet searches and getting millions of Web sites in the results, including many commercial sites. It can be difficult to discern what is trustworthy and what is not.

There is a quick and easy tactic that can help you nearly eliminate the pesky glut of commercial Web sites from a search with just one click. This tactic is called "The Minus Dot Com Trick." In this tactic, add a minus sign (or a hyphen) and the word ".com" to your search word. For example, one search might read: "jobs. com"

If you go to Google today and try this on the word jobs, you will find the number of results go from an astounding 937 million pages of results to 382 million pages or results—nearly a 61 percent reduction—in one click. It works because the minus sign tells the search engine to ignore Web sites with ".com" (or, commercial sites) and therefore focus your results on educational or government Web sites, which are much more trustworthy. This powerful technique works on just about any key search word at any major search engine online.

The next search trick is to use more words in your search. But what words do you use? Focus on words associated with job search skills and the key documents you need to use. Use "job search" as the first two words in your search query. Now add a subtopic, such as "résumé writing." When you submit this four-word search query—"Job search résumé writing"—the search engine finds Web pages that have all four words.

Then, to find examples of résumés other people have used, you can use the key words "examples" or "samples." The results of this five-word search will get you to numerous résumé samples after which you can model your own.

Add words for the subjects you are interested in or have experience and qualifications. Try "computers," "medical," or "construction." This six-word search will narrow the results even more. The more words you use, the more focused results you will obtain.

One of the best techniques to use on an Internet search is to search for types of companies by location. There are even specialized search engines that can help you. Google Maps is a powerful tool that you can use to identify actual companies and their addresses and phone numbers in your local area. For example, if you wanted to identify the locations of engineering firms in a certain city, enter your town or city into Google Maps. Then enter the keywords for the type of business. The results you get will create a virtual roadmap of potential employers for you to visit.

My daughter used this technique to get a summer intern job at an engineering company last summer. She used Google Maps and entered the words "Engineering Richland, WA." Over a two week period, she dropped off a résumé and letter at twenty-five companies. She ended up with a several interviews and an offer for a great summer job with a federal government contractor.

Using the Internet to post vast numbers of résumés can be a colossal waste of time. Rather than blasting résumés out via e-mail, use the Web to research first and then network. Do not just search for jobs. Look for people with problems you can solve. You have to connect with real people in a meaningful way. Search for opportunities in the areas that you love—hobbies, sports, special interests, and skill areas. Then, talk to the people you encounter as you find information. Contact them and set up a face-to-face meeting, conduct an informational interview, ask questions, and follow up on what you learn. This is how to really use the Internet.

Researching and Profiling Potential Employers

Targeting specific companies during your job search is one of the most effective ways you can spend your time. Profiling and researching your targeted group of employers takes an investment of time on your part, but the dividends are high.

Here are some things you will want to learn from your research:

- How well is the company doing within its competitive market(s)? Is it a leader? If not, why? Is it profitable? If not, why?
- What are the most profitable areas of the company?
- Which areas have contributed the most to overall growth of the company?
- What are the key drivers of the business?
- Where is the company making investments for future growth and profits?
- What do stock analysts (if it is a publicly-traded company) think of its future prospects?
- What comes up when you Google the company's name?
- If you scan the last six months of news archives, what are the items that pop up about this company?
- Who are the key officers who run the company?
- What are bloggers saying about the company?
- What is it like to work for the company? What kind of culture does it have?
- Does the website have a job posting board?
- What is the hiring process? Who are the company recruiters? What outside firms have provided recruiting services to the company?
- Who are the hiring managers in this field of expertise?

Ask these and many more questions about a particular company during your job search. The key point here is to use information that most people pass by to find "data clues" that can help you during your job search. Let's take a look at ways and methods you can scan for data clues.

Use the News

Both online and offline sources of news can be scanned to find the kinds of data that you can leverage during your search. Online scanning is easy enough these days. Most search engines, such as Google, allow you to set up news searches on any topic. This includes looking for newsworthy items from all over the globe on a targeted company.

The first step in scanning news items is to set up news alerts. For example, in Google you can set up an alert by simply using keywords or company name; specifying how wide or narrow you want to conduct your news searches (scanning just blogs, Web sites, news services, online video, or groups). The comprehensive selection gives you the widest and best range of news items on your target area. You can also select the frequency in which you want to receive feeds on either a daily or weekly basis.

If you can, it may pay for you to invest in the trade magazines that cover your industry. Industry periodicals can be a very valuable source of information. Remember, all your research efforts should be aimed at two specific goals: 1) to find job leads and 2) to find additional people to network with during your search.

Here are items you should be scanning for:

- News about products and services. New products, revamped products, and products that are fueling growth are key items. These are telltale signs that a company may be hiring and expanding in a specific area of the firm.

- Names of specific managers and key officers. Many times the news media mentions people who work for the company, usually key people who are involved in whatever level of news is being generated on the company.

- Expansion plans. Look for any news that talks about new company investments or new projects, products, and services can give you insights and clues as to what is happening at a company. You want to target those areas of a company that are profitable and growing. Are they generating jobs though all this news?

- News about people who work for the company. This can help you find potential networking contacts. Anytime you find the name of a manager or officer at a target company, check the person out on online networks, such as LinkedIn or Facebook. Does the person have an online profile? If he does, you have just found a way to potentially network with the contact or, even better, the people in the contact's network. In LinkedIn, for example, you can generally see people's connections. You are more than likely going to find other people within the company that are already in the LinkedIn network. Rule of thumb: anytime you find a contact name, run it through the online networking engines.

Scanning Annual Reports

A great and often underutilized source of job search information is the company annual report. The job searcher who targets specific companies for job leads and opportunities will be more effective in his search than someone who is attempting to mass market himself. An annual report on your targeted company may reveal the following kinds of information:

- Divisions of the company that are expanding via sales growth and/or direct investment for future growth (read: job opportunities).
- New products and services being developed to help drive current and future growth (more job opportunities).

- Key personnel who are highlighted because of the importance of their work to the company.
- Mergers and acquisitions that occurred during the year. What impact do these activities have on the company and the potential for job opportunities with those acquired companies?

Every annual report will be structured a bit differently and vary in the amounts of soft information it contains. "Soft information" is non-financial data and is usually commentary contained in the annual report that reflects their current and future strategies and opportunities that the company sees for itself.

If your target company is public, then the basis of your research on the company should be built partly on the content in annual reports. You can find the annual shareholder reports many publicly-traded companies by utilizing Internet resources, such as www.annualreportservice.com.

The Inc. Magazine 500: A Job Seeker's Research Tool

Every year, *Inc.* magazine (www.inc.com) publishes a list of the 500 fastest-growing private companies in the United States. It contains a treasure trove of information that can provide valuable insights on business strategy and tactics. This is a list of 500 medium-sized businesses that are in the thick of executing on business strategies that are differentiating them from their baseline competitors.

Inc. has segmented companies in this list into broad but meaningful sectors, such as media, business services, construction, education, logistics, retail, transportation, etc. If you are targeting a specific industry for job leads or networking opportunities, it is probably listed here.

Finding and reviewing your sector is a great place to start when researching this publication. Here are some basic questions that can often be answered by using the *Inc. 500* issue:

What are some of these high growth companies in your sector doing strategically and/or tactically to position themselves as high-performers?

How is the company creating differentiation that separates it from the crowd?

The company's performance record is not always featured in the magazine. However, there is great information on each company that you can use to your benefit in your job search. For instance, *Inc.* gives you the CEO's name and the company's Web site address. Use this information as a starting off point for your search.

At a minimum, your research will require a careful and detailed review of the company's Web site. Then, follow up with a call to the company if you want to find out more information. You would be surprised how much information you can get if you just pick up the phone and call the CEO directly.

Remember, the CEOs featured in this magazine are not Fortune 500 CEOs; rather, these CEOs are generally much more accessible. You can usually find someone at the management level of a company who is willing to brag about his firm.

Here are some key questions to ask about each company you review:

- What is it about these companies that make them qualify for the *Inc. 500*? What are they excelling at that allows them to create opportunities to grow profitably?
- What are the major trends that show up within companies in the category? What are the critical factors that drive the industry based on what you see in the *Inc. 500* list?
- Is the growth organic (growth based on internal investment in the business) or synthetic growth (growth built on acquisitions)?

- What is the company's story? How did the company grow? How long has the company been in business? If it has a Web site, you can usually find its story there.
- Who are the key decision makers in hiring? Is the company hiring? Does it list career opportunities on its Web site?
- What has been the trend in the company's latest news or press releases?
- What can you find out about the company by Googling its name? This includes each of the officers of the corporation.
- Does the company have a blog? Blogs can be a key way to get a read on the latest issues that a company is concerned about and/or dealing with. It is also a great way to see how people outside of the company interact and the types of dialogue that develop in a company blog. What is being said on the blog? What are other customers or clients saying on the blogs?
- How does the company utilize its Web site? Does it update its sales, product info, and industry-oriented content? What does it emphasize on its homepage?

If trying to target growing companies for job opportunities, the *Inc. 500* listing is a great way to garner some valuable and usable insights. This kind of ranking process offers those who are willing to invest some time a strategic way to determine what kinds of businesses might be on the short list of consideration.

Recruitment Firms

Recruitment firms are in business to do one thing: place mid-to-higher levels managers and technical experts into the firms that the firms represent. Most recruiters work off of a percentage of a new hires base salary after the new candidate has been placed. Whatever their compensation, recruiters remain a steadfast source of unadvertised positions. Many companies, both large and small, will utilize the services of a recruitment firm when they have a critical position to fill.

Recruiters are a wealth of knowledge, which is particularly important in very specialized areas of expertise. Here are some tips for managing and expanding recruitment relationships in order to expand both the reach and depth of your research prowess:

1. Create a separate database for recruiters. This is a good group to keep separate from other groups. Learn as much about them as you can during the course of phone conversations, e-mails, and tweets. Even with quite a bit of turnover in this field, the good and well-connected ones seem to remain top performers in the field for many years. Those are the recruiters you want to target during your job search campaign.

2. Always be helpful in the recruitment process. Even if you are not interested in the position they are pitching you, make every attempt to help them identify viable contacts from your own network list. Recruiters never forget that kind of assistance.

3. Pick their brains for ideas. As you start to develop a relationship with a core group of recruiters, you have a good window of opportunity to chat with them every now and then, preferably by phone. This is a great research opportunity for you. What kinds of positions do they see more often these days? What parts of the United States are still generating recruitment projects? What kinds of firms are still active or more active than most companies? What resources would they recommend you use to aid you in your search to generate more job opportunities? You cannot ask these kinds of questions cold, but as you develop a relationship with recruiters, do not forget to leverage what they know to your advantage.

4. Target the right recruiters. There is something to be said for targeting the right recruiters. That means seeking out, locating, and targeting recruiters that have expertise in your field. If you are a chemical engineer, for instance, you should target and focus on recruiters who are fully or at least partially engaged in recruitment projects in that field. The more specialized the recruiter, the better for you.

5. Always say thank you. Make it a point to send a personalized thank you note anytime a recruiter lends an ear and/or provides some insights for you to consider. This is obviously true when they call you to see if you are interested in a position they are actively seeking to fill.

6. Keep your professional information updated. It is easy to let time go by and end up with stale information sitting on the databases of multiple recruiters from a number of firms. Any time you have a change or update, make sure your recruiter has it, too.

7. Constantly scan the media and your network contacts for new recruitment resources and contacts. There are literally thousands of recruitment firms of all sizes and specialties out there. Make it a point to research and make contact with some new firms each week. You can never have enough recruiters in your contact database.

Expert Insights with Tom Dimmick

Tom is a twenty-five year veteran of the corporate HR world where he rose to a division VP position in a Fortune 100 firm before going out on his own and founding DK Search, Inc. (www.dksearchinc. com). You can reach him at tom@dksearchinc.com.

Dirks: What skills does someone need today in order to be highly effective during a job search? Why is each skill critical to building a successful job search campaign?

Dimmick: The skills that people need today are really no different than they have ever been. In my opinion, it really is not a matter of any particular set of skills but rather some behaviors that are essential. The behaviors that I believe are required are: self knowledge, focus, patience, and persistence.

· Self-knowledge: Candidates must understand that they are not qualified for every position. That sounds very basic, but it really is quite profound as it sets the framework for a variety of other behaviors. Candidates must know what they are good at doing and where they have shortcomings. They must know what kinds of organizations play to those strong suits and what kinds do not. For example, a candidate from GM's group of procurement people has a very different and completely unsuited set of experiences for an opportunity in a $50 million dollar manufacturing organization. The infrastructure is different, the support systems are different, and the accountabilities are different. More importantly, the manner in which the work is performed is different.

- Focus: Once self knowledge has really become foundational, the candidate needs to remain focused only on those opportunities that will result in a good fit with a new organization. Can a person make a transition from a large corporation to a small one? Maybe, but employers are risk adverse. With all of the candidates on the market today and the scarcity of jobs, candidates need to remain focused on where they have the greatest likelihood of success.

- Patience: Companies do not move at the speed candidates might like. There are many dynamics to the hiring process and all kinds of competing elements for a hiring manager's time and attention. It does no good to become frustrated with the recruiter, the HR department, or the hiring manager. Set reasonable expectations whenever possible but do not become overly distraught when things take longer than you have thought or been told.

- Persistence: In spite of rejections, in spite of frustrations, the candidate must be persistent in his efforts to re-enter the job market. When a candidate is employed, he is sought by competitors and others. When he is unemployed, he must do the seeking, and he must be persistent in developing new network contacts and means of uncovering opportunities.

Dirks: What are five common mistakes made by people who utilize executive recruiters (and recruiters in general), and what should they do differently?

Dimmick: There are many more than five common mistakes, but I will give you the four that I believe are the most detrimental to a candidate's success in finding a new position.

- Failure to understand the hiring process: This is perhaps the single greatest failure that a candidate can make. Candidates must clearly understand the difference in methodology and approach between a contingent search and a retained search. The fee payment has a huge impact on the hiring process and candidates need to understand what the impact is on them. The requirement for speed for a contingent recruiter is far different than it is for a retained recruiter. Similarly, the dynamics of the relationship between the recruiter and the client is very different for a retained recruiter than it is for a contingent recruiter. Candidates need to be able to understand the dynamics and work within them.

- Failure to position: This refers back to the self-knowledge element mentioned earlier. Candidates must know and understand which recruiters they want to deal with and what they can expect from those recruiters. Candidates cannot go to a sales focused recruiter and expect that they will properly represent them in their search for a nursing position.

- Failure to investigate: There is so much information available today that it is inexcusable for a candidate not to know and understand what the search firm of his choice will and will not do on his behalf. Candidates must accept the idea that they are not the client. The recruiter, whether it is a retained or a contingent recruiter, is driven by the fee. In nearly every case, the fee is paid by the employer and that makes the employer the client, not the candidate.

- Failure to maintain enthusiasm: Candidates must not fall into the mindset that they can control the process or control the outcome. That is simply not so. The only time the candidate has the decision in his hands is when an offer has been presented. However; a candidate can and must give continual evidence of a genuine enthusiasm in the position. If he does not do so, the recruiter will pick up on that shift and refocus his own efforts to present a candidate that has a greater likelihood of appeal to the client.

Dirks: What strategies and tactics are recruiters using today to find the best candidates?

Dimmick: The Internet has had a huge impact on recruiting. The number of job boards, subscription services, and social networkers on the Internet has made candidate identification far more rapid. The social networking sites in particular (i.e., LinkedIn, YouTube, and Facebook), has given recruiters a glimpse into the lives of active and passive candidates that did not exist five years ago. Candidates need to remember that the cute outfit they wore to that party may be completely inappropriate when viewed by a potential employer. Recruiters must be actively engaged in doing the kind of research that best protects the interests of their clients. Recruiters now research huge amounts of data to verify work histories, publications, and awards in addition to fit.

Assessment has also become a very common tool for employers. There are scores of online testing services that will provide a potential employer or recruiter with a very accurate description of the working style of the candidate. Prices range from a few hundred dollars to several thousand dollars, depending upon the complexity of the testing. The candidate can plan on spending several hours to several days to complete such an assessment and may have little feedback given to him if the client is footing the testing bill.

Dirks: What other comments/suggestions would you have for the person undertaking a job search campaign?

Dimmick: The comment and suggestion that I have for potential candidates can be easily summarized and is simple: *Do not take it personally!* The recruiting process is not straightforward. It is not easily defined and cannot be controlled by the candidate. While that does not excuse a candidate from failing to clearly know what he can and cannot do well, from failing to do diligent research on the recruiter and the client firm, it does mean that he should never let the episodes he experiences defeat him.

Temporary Employment Agencies

A very traditional way of getting work, creating income, and potentially finding another job has been going the temporary agency route. For nonexecutive positions, this still has some potential. There are plenty of companies who hire temporary employees to fill what is thought at the time to be just "temporary" needs. However, there are times when firms will decide to make a particular temporary position a more "permanent" one (that term is used loosely as there is no such thing as "permanent" work anywhere). It is also possible that, after a period of demonstrating your expertise and skills, employers determine that you are a valuable asset and offer you a position.

If for nothing else, temporary agencies can be a good source for researching the career areas that seem to trend positively. You may find some of the larger agencies publishing white papers on specialty subjects related to your industry or career track.

Expert Insights with Phil Collins

Phil Collins has thirty years experience as a recruiter and search firm owner. He is the founder and managing partner of Claremont-Branan Group, LLC, an employment services firm. Check out his Web site at www.ontheoffensejobsearch.com. He can be reached at phil@c-bgroup.com.

Dirks: What skills does someone need today in order to be highly effective during a job search? Why are these skills critical to building a successful job search campaign?

Collins: *A sense of direction*: Most importantly, job seekers need to decide what it is they want to do. The immediate reaction to being without a job is to go online, look at job boards, and begin to fire off résumés. Without establishing a focused direction early in their process, too much time will be wasted going after the wrong thing.

The ability to focus: Searching for a job requires the ability to focus on your goal and to apply your efforts toward achieving success; in this case, your next position.

Research skills: Upon establishing a direction, the job seeker will benefit by having the ability to find information which will lead him to "buyers" of his skills.

Communications skills: Upon deciding their goals, exact objectives, successful job seekers will be able to communicate this objective in clear and concise terms to anyone who will listen. Equally important is their ability to convey this information in written form.

Organizational skills: Successful job seekers require good organizational skills. Schedule, plan, execute, and follow up. You are in charge of your time, and you are the project manager of your own job search. Make to-do lists. Create a daily plan; set goals and record your progress.

Dirks: What are five common mistakes made by people who utilize executive recruiters (and recruiters in general), and what should they do differently?

Collins: *Misunderstanding the nature of the recruiting business*: Executive recruiters find qualified candidates for their clients. For the most part, they do not find jobs for candidates.

Attempting to work with recruiters who have no experience with your industry, or experience at all: Take the time to locate and screen recruiters based upon their knowledge and experience in your industry.

Failure to convey a sense of direction: An executive recruiter will be more inclined to present a candidate to a client for consideration if the candidate has a good understanding of his employment goal, strengths and weaknesses, and appropriate understanding of where his skills can be best employed.

Withholding information: Be truthful with recruiters. If you cannot accept a relocation, let them know. If you have a minimum base salary requirement, tell them. If they ask about your most recent compensation plan, tell them everything. If you do not feel comfortable sharing this with a recruiter, do not work with one.

Handing over control of your résumé: While you should be truthful with a recruiter, you should also expect cooperation from him. Insist that a recruiter get your permission before sharing your résumé with any of his clients. The last thing you, or the recruiter, needs is to send your résumé to a company only to find that it had been previously submitted.

Dirks: What strategies and tactics are recruiters using today to find the best candidates?

Collins: Advertising: Unfortunately, some recruiters rely heavily on the major job search engines and niche job boards to find candidates. They forego passive candidate identification techniques and rely heavily on résumé traffic from active candidates placing advertisements or searching the site's résumé database.

Network membership: Many recruiters participate in formal and informal networks of fellow recruiters where job postings and résumés are shared in an environment conducive to making "splits," the equivalent to the relationship that real estate agents have when one party represents the "seller" and one party represents the "buyer" and fees are split according to a prearranged (typically 50/50) basis.

Social and business networking sites: The current trend finds recruiters participating in the various online social and/or business networking sites. Logically, these Web sites are a recruiter's playground. With basic research techniques, a good recruiter, or his researcher, can identify prospective contacts (candidates and employers) on these sites. Moreover, an active sub-industry exists with the goal of training recruiters to use these networks with greater effectiveness.

Old fashioned research: Many recruiters, either on their own or in conjunction with an in-house or third-party researcher, continue to rely on basic research techniques to drive passive candidate identification processes. These "in the trenches" strategies use various techniques to identify currently employed candidates who are performing the role for which their client has hired them to recruit. These truly passive candidates are not registered on job boards and, believe it or not, may not have a profile on Linkedin or
Facebook.

Dirks: What other comments/suggestions would you have for the person undertaking a job search campaign?

Collins: Take the time to decide exactly what you want to do. There are a number of problem-solving techniques you can use to accomplish this. Once you have a direction, you are better able to equip your network to help you, and your self-confidence level soars, as well. Only when you know where you are going can you craft a good "elevator speech."

- Do not rely solely on your computer and the Internet! With your goal in mind, first identify prospective employers, their suppliers, vendors, and customers; all of whom may represent entry points for you to consider.

- Try to find out who makes decisions, then devise an approach that will put you in direct contact with them.

- Do not rely on submitting résumés to human resources based upon a company's job posting Web site, especially when targeting potential employers at the top of your list.

- Be patient, yet persistent. Do not forget to touch base with your network every few weeks by e-mail or phone to let the network know of your progress; remind the network of your goal and keep your name and interests in front of it. People forget unless reminded.

- Organize your efforts and keep records of contacts, résumés sent, results and follow up action required.

- Customize your résumé specifically for every position to which you apply.

- Reach out to friends and family; do not withdraw. Look for ways to have fun; volunteer, exercise, and/or participate in group sports. Looking for a job is mentally and physically stressful. You need outlets, so find and use them.

The Chamber of Commerce

In Chapter 8, The Face of Networking: Traditional Face-to-Face, I noted that your local Chamber of Commerce was a great place to begin networking into the local business community. It is also a great source of research information that can potentially help you in your search for job opportunities.

Most local Chambers put out a monthly publication that showcases new businesses in the area as well as other potentially important business news and events. You need to get a copy of that publication and scan it every month for potential information that could lead to more network contacts and job leads. Who is opening a new business? Who is expanding one? What Chamber networking opportunities are open this month?

Commercial Phone Directories

Commercial phone book directories make a great research tool. They are usually a good place to start during the initial stages of your job search campaign when you are looking for likely businesses to investigate for potential job leads or, at the least, networking opportunities. That said, the commercial phone directories or books like it, are not effective if you do not pick up the phone and call companies to find out what they are up to or if they know of someone who might be able to help you.

Newspaper Classifieds

While they are not nearly what they once were to job seekers, the newspaper classified sections, especially in the Wednesday and Sunday editions of the papers (where the job ad count is generally the highest), are at least worth a few minutes of your time each day. With page counts down dramatically in these one-time icons of the job search campaign, it will not take you long to scan the classified section for any potential. It may spark an idea or at least potentially connect you with someone within the firm who you could network with. Everything has networking possibilities these days.

Becoming a proficient researcher using both online and offline resources is one of the lesser known keys to job search success. Knowing how and where to obtain the information you will need to accelerate your job search campaign is critical. The faster you can obtain the information you need to be effective, the shorter the cycle time it will take to generate career opportunities.

Chapter 11
Developing Your Personal Brand

Personal brand: The art of managing the professional and personal perceptions that people have about you. A personal brand is built on the foundation of how people perceive you. A great measure of your success in finding job opportunities will be based on how well you develop and present your personal brand to the world. Personal branding has become the centerpiece for modern job search campaigns. Your personal brand is also an evolving, growing component of your career and lives well beyond the confines of the occasional job search campaign.

There has been a lot of excitement in the last few years in the media about the concept of personal branding. The truth is personal branding is a concept that has been around forever. There have always been a small percentage of career professionals who understood how to package, market, and position themselves in the job marketplace. They were distinctly noted as people of "great reputation." People knew what these professionals stood for and could count on them to deliver on that reputation every time.

Today, more people have been studying these methods and put them into the context of modern corporate branding but apply them at the personal level.

There have been some excellent books written on the topic of personal branding and you will find some of them listed in the resource section of this book. Here is how you can put personal branding within the context of job search marketing.

We live in an era of business turbulence. It is a cycle of seemingly constant change. Gone are the days when you could work for a company doing just one job. Today, more and more employers deal with a high level of rapid change by moving people around and getting them to adapt to different work teams and assignments. Amidst this swirl of change there has to be one thing that remains steady and dependable: your personal brand.

Employers in today's job market look for people who can adapt to rapid change but still deliver on certain defined results. Your personal brand allows you to constantly project what you stand for and can deliver to your employer. It is a way to position yourself against any competition and win.

That only happens if you have a brand reputation that is worth looking at. Just step back for a moment and you can probably think of people who have excellent reputations. Just the mention of their names conjures up certain images of quality or excellence. They are the people who are able to differentiate themselves from their competitors based on the strength of their personal brand. They are credible and authentic. People are compelled to listen to them because their personal brand stands for something.

Expert Insights with Dan Schawbel

Dan Schawbel is the leading personal branding expert for Gen-Y. He is the Dan Schawbel author of the bestselling career book, Me 2.0: Build a Powerful Brand to Achieve Career Success (Kaplan, April 2009). Check out his Web site at www.DanSchawbel.com.

Dirks: In the context of conducting a job search, why should someone be concerned about developing and presenting his personal brand?

Schawbel: We are already branded by the people that surround us. In order to have a successful job search, we must understand our brand and how we want to be positioned in the marketplace, relative to everyone else. Most people do not find the right career path because they do not understand where they fit into the world, what skills they really have to offer, and what they are passionate about. You should be concerned about how you dress, your behavior and how you build your online brand. Everything should be consistent and it should be reflective of the audience you want to target. For instance, you should not put up pictures or update your status messages with things you are not proud of or do not want to show publicly.

Dirks: What are some ways that personal branding can be integrated into the job search process and why?

Schawbel: Every Web site that holds your name is part of your personal brand. You have the opportunity to build your brand for free now using mass distribution systems, such as YouTube, blogs, and social networks. By using these channels, you are able to project your value to thousands of people in a very short period of time without having to break open your piggy bank. Using the Web to get a job is a requirement in this digital world. Since recruiters are already searching your name (and for people like you) on LinkedIn and Facebook, you better be positioned right and have your profiles there.

Also, your name, picture, and personal brand statement (what you do and who you serve) should be on all of your Web sites, your résumé, and other materials. Personal branding must be integrated into your job search because everything you touch is part of your brand, and you will be judged based on what people read about you and how you package it (and how you tell your story).

Dirks: How can ignoring your personal brand possibly affect the outcome of your job search campaign?

Schawbel: You will end up at the wrong company in the wrong position. You may also change jobs and/or careers too many times in your lifetime because you did not take the time to discover your passion and execute it. By not building your profile online, you miss opportunities every day. Also, personal branding differentiates individuals. If you avoid it, then you will be more of a commodity and you may miss out on hiring opportunities at premium pay.

Dirks: How can personal branding as a concept help the job seeker to differentiate himself in a very competitive job market?

Schawbel: Personal branding forces you to be the best at something for a specific audience. It is not to say that generalists will not be successful, but if you do not specialize in something, it will be very hard to be successful. Personal branding teaches you to be yourself instead of copying others because your personality is your greatest asset and cannot be stolen from you.

Dirks: Give three common mistakes you see most people make when it comes to developing, nurturing, and marketing their personal brand?

Schawbel: Most people are too aggressive with self-promotion. For instance, they will leave long signatures when they comment on blogs, obnoxious e-mail signatures, and four page bios on their Web sites. These things can turn people off immediately. Another mistake people make is that they fail to discover their personal brand before they create the materials around it. You need to know where you are and where you are going before you start creating content to reflect that. The third mistake I see is that people do not understand the importance of claiming their online identities, such as registering their domain name (yourname.com). If you do not register your name, someone else might and you will lose opportunities.

Dirks: Any other comments/suggestions that you would have for people who are undertaking a job search campaign as it relates to personal branding?

Schawbel: I would suggest that they decide what industry they want to go in and then locate the social networks that cater to those industries online, join them, and become active participants.

I suggest having a focused job search, so that they are only looking at the top three companies where they want to work. Then conduct a people search online to find people that work at those companies. Finally, remember to work as hard as you can to become friends with these potential contacts and then ask for a job.

To start the process of determining your personal brand, try this exercise:

1. Sit down in a quiet place where you will not be distracted.

2. For each job position you have had over the last five to ten years, make a list of every project, contribution, and idea you have had. You are simply brainstorming here so do not evaluate this list; just list as many achievements as possible. Include accomplishments from any nonprofit activities, as well, especially where held a leadership position. Use this list of projects, contributions, and ideas to help you identify what differentiates you from your potential competitors.

Here are some things to consider when either establishing or building your personal brand:

1. Personal branding is about the images you convey to people. It is the messages that you project to people when you meet them or when they see your work. It is about the way you interact with people in a professional environment. Your personal brand is largely determined by the opinion people have of you.

2. Be absolutely honest with yourself about the current health of your personal brand. You will gain nothing by trying to fool yourself into thinking you are one thing when the reality of what others think of you is quite different. If there is

a wide variance between what you think your brand reputation is and the reality of what it is, you will be found out in short order. This is absolutely critical. Your brand is your reputation. Do not screw it up and if you do, fix it right away and move on from there.

3.	Personal brands are not built overnight. Your personal brand is crafted and honed during years of business experience.

4.	Ask yourself: What are your career goals and ambitions? Are they still the same as when you started or have they changed? What has changed about your career goals? The point is to have a clear assessment of your goals. If your career goals are in a state of flux (i.e., you are an investment banker thinking of changing careers and going into nursing), you will need to be clear about the objective of your job search.

5.In the context of job search marketing, we have to deal with what your brand is right now. Unless you are independently wealthy, you do not have years to either build or rebuild a reputation. You have to deal with what it is right now.

6.Ask your colleagues, your manager (and previous managers), and friends what words come to mind when they think of you in the professional environment? What words are they using and how?

7.Think of your personal brand as a list of features and benefits about you. Your brand features are those things about which you know and have expertise. Your brand benefits are those things that you excel in doing or producing.

Try this exercise:

1. Make a list of brand features directly related to your career and write a corresponding benefit for each feature you list. We will call this your "features and benefits" list.

Example: Feature: Excellent project management skills; Benefit: Brings projects to completion on time and under budget.

2. Using the information you learned here and in the Your Marketability Assessment chapter and the features and benefits list you completed above, boil the information down to one key thing that your potential employers should think of when they see or hear about you.

Example: *My personal brand: I create and deliver innovative and profitable marketing strategies that are designed to drive business growth.*

Once you can clearly and concisely define your personal brand in one statement, the next part is injecting your brand into everything you do during your job search. This includes adding it to your business cards, your résumé, letterhead, your personal Web site, blog, and all other digital and print collateral that is connected to you. Integrate your personal brand down to things like your Facebook, Linkedin, and MySpace sites.

Integrating your personal brand into everything you do ensures that every networking contact, referral source, and potential employer sees your brand attributes clearly and understands them. During the course of your job search, people need to know what you stand for. Your brand reputation must be seen and felt at all times and in all things you do.

Your personal brand can be distributed in a wide number of ways these days: one-on-one networking, web-based networks (i.e., Linkedin, Facebook), personal Web sites, Weblogs, podcasting, business cards, letterhead, vodcasting (video podcasting), newsletters, e-mail campaigns, your résumé, and many other kinds of personal brand collateral. Use as many distribution channels as possible to get as much personal brand exposure as possible.

Get a professionally done photograph of you to use on all of your distribution channels, and ditch any photos that are less than professional. For just a few bucks, you can get a professional-looking series of photos that will be appropriate for the Web, press releases, or any other job search collateral you might create and use.

Expert Insights with Steven Van Yoder, author of *Get Slightly Famous*

Steven Van Yoder (www.getslightlyfamous.com) is a seasoned journalist, published in over 200 publications including The Washington Post, Financial Executive, Home Office Computing, Costco Connection, Industry Week, Brand Marketing, and dozens of trade, business and consumer publications.

Drawing from years of experience as a working journalist, Steven uses his inside understanding of targeted PR strategies to help small businesses reach their best clients and customers and develop a unique brand identity, and harness the media to become recognized leaders in their industries.

You can reach him at steven@getslightlyfamous.com

Dirks: In the context of a job search campaign, why is it important to take the time and care to develop a personal brand?

Van Yoder: It is especially important in a job market like the one we are facing now and I predict we will be facing for many years. The job market is a very competitive place when it comes to getting a job and advancing your career. You need to do anything you can to build a "value-add" to your overall proposition in the eyes of potential employers. When there are more and more people standing in line looking for the same job, it is going to be the extra (or value-added) things. These are more than just a few bullet points on a piece of paper (like your résumé).

We are talking about reputation that may precede you or reputation and credibility that you can point to. Increasingly, this process is being lead by the Internet and Web 2.0. Employers do use Google to check candidates out before they hire them. What they find out about you on the Internet is how they rank you and move you to the top of the list. If you are a fairly anonymous, middle manager that has been in a particular industry and have moved through various positions over the course of ten years, employers should see that progression. They should see what you are currently doing and leadership initiatives you are taking within your particular industry.

There is a premise here that by developing your reputation (personal brand) in your space (industry, career-specialty, etc.), you are on a career path already. You need to demonstrate your leadership and expertise in your particular space of interest. It means showing that you add more value than just doing your job and getting a paycheck. You need to develop a reputation that precedes you and where more and more people know what you do. When it comes time to look for a job, you have a network of people you already have a relationship with.

You have to anticipate in business, what I call your "virtual first impression." When your résumé or your job application is being considered and the hiring managers go to Google and start looking for you, already you should have deliberately thought through and created the kind of impression you want them to find on Google search results.

There are several ways to create a positive virtual first impression. One way is to have your own personal Web presence. You can do this in a variety of ways. It is fairly easy to set up a simple website and sometimes for free. It is easy to set up profiles on social networking sites such as Linkedin and Facebook. So the point is to deliberately create a Web presence and not let it happen on its own. You need to cultivate the kind of reputation on the Web that you want people to find when the Google you. Whatever Web platform you use, it should showcase your career accomplishments, your capabilities, and it should show that you are contributing in a broader way to your industry (or career area).

Dirks: Why is focusing on a specific industry, company, or companies during a more effective way to create the personal branding and differentiation you need to stand out in a crowded job market?

Van Yoder: Look at it from a business-to-business 'Get Slightly Famous' perspective. Let's say you are a management consultant and you are looking to expand your business and trying to be everything to everybody. Stop. I say you need to pick and industry by looking at your best clients. Let's also say that your best clients are in the construction industry.

Using the Get Slightly Famous process, you would get "famous" within that industry and build your business around attracting more of them. You do not want to be a management consultant for everybody, which effectively means everybody but nobody. In this case, you would want to be the management consultant in the industry that speaks the language and presents thought-leadership around the construction industry. That would be a typical Get Slightly Famous strategy.

What makes you special? Is it what you do or is it the industry focus that you can cultivate that will make you special and differentiate yourself from your competition? The latter position makes you much more relevant and allows you to easily build a Get Slightly Famous marketing strategy.

If you were a marketer within the tech industry, you would want to focus your long-term job and career path within the tech industry, your focus would be to have a targeted approach. Within the tech industry you could segment even further. For example, you might look at the software area versus the semiconductor tech area. Once you are able to narrow your focus, you can then get the layout of the industry. Once you drill down to specific industries, it is easier to research their blogs, conferences, white papers, associations, and Web sites where industry people congregate and share information. You really need to have a 360-degree view of your particular industry focus.

You also need to identify the people who are known within an industry as "influencers." Increasingly, there are more and more people who are influencers within an industry, and you can find them online.

The trade media is another place to find information and contacts that you can relate to your job search. Your local library will usually give you access to the specific trade media or where to at least find them.

You want to have a good list of all those things that influence an industry. You have the places identified where people stay current with conferences, blogs, etc.

With this information in hand, you start following those industries. You subscribe to some trade publications and begin reading industry blogs on a regular basis. Then it is important to start participating and start to position yourself as a center of influence.

Online one of the easiest ways to do that is to follow blogs, and once you have a good idea of an influential bloggers slant or viewpoint, start joining in on the discussions and comments. Start looking for other people who are following those blogs and have a level of influence in them. Get connected to these people. Develop visibility for yourself within that industry by having your name, title, and an easy-to-remember and compelling tagline and biography go along with all of the participation you do in that industry.

So the Get Slightly Famous strategy in the job search context would be to find, read, follow, and participate in online discussions. Go out of your way to connect with the centers of influence with the industry.

Dirks: How is thought leadership important to a job search campaign?

Van Yoder: What is a thought leader? That is somebody who is participating in and ultimately shaping in some way the ongoing discussions within one particular industry. Why do that? You do it because it is a value-add to your personal brand. If there are ten people being considered for a position, nine of those people consist of two pages of accomplishments on a résumé. If you are that tenth person, you have an accomplished résumé; an online presence; and you are connected people who are influencing the industry, and you have earned a level of trust and respect within those circles.

With a blog, it is easy to see who reads it and you can point to it so other people can find it. The connections that you develop just from blogging will give you a deeper and richer experience. If someone hires you, bring along all of your accomplishments and connections in the service of your job. This makes you a much more valuable employee.

You are also noted as someone who thinks strategically about yourself, which implies that you will think strategically about advancing the company's agenda, as well. Thought leadership really makes you an entrepreneur. Thought leaders demonstrate a level of initiative that is often rare among employees. Most people are very passive about this.

Another way to become a thought leader is to start writing short articles. These articles do not have to be major productions. You can write informative and valuable articles that can then be posted to Web sites that welcome outside copy. Just make sure you get clear credit for the article and you include a bio box and a link to your Web site and/or blog. When you start doing this, you will find that search engines, such as Google, will begin to pick up these articles; they come up in searches under your name.

Trade publications are always hungry for contributors. You do not have to be a journalist to get an article published in a trade publication. Understand the publication's content and develop articles that are a fit within that publication. There is nothing that shouts credibility more than an article that has your name on it. It is entirely realistic and possible to pursue this writing route.

The more you can cultivate more of this thought leadership, the more you appear as a desirable person to know. People will want to know you.

Dirks: How does networking fit into the job search campaign and why is it important?

Van Yoder: Relationships are everything. The old saying is "dig your well before you need it." Cultivating a networking of people within your industry and outside of it should be a key strategy in professional life.

The more you can weave and connect your bottom line with others, the more people will help you. This assumes that you have giving relationships as well. Sometimes people forget that. Most people do not appreciate other people who are interested in just taking from a relationship.

For both live and online networking situations, start with a clear strategy of getting connected with the types of people that you want to meet. There is a strategic part of this where you want to be connected to people that have their own deep networks. If you are connected to a particular industry, you should look at all the things you can do in your business life to cultivate that first level of networking. That first level of networking opens itself up to additional levels of relationships and your network continues to grow and flourish.

Another strategy to help you broaden and deepen your networking is to join groups. LinkedIn is an excellent example of a place where you can link to individuals and groups. Search and look for the groups that influence and build followings within LinkedIn about different industry discussions. If you are into software, you should look around and subscribe to software groups that are likely to have conversations and the people that are driving those conversations. If you become a participant in those conversations, you can really begin to expand your network.

Your reputation is not only important but mobile. It is possible to plant "reputation seeds" and develop relationships with people all over the country and the world in your industry. These are the relationships that can be leveraged when you are in a job search.

For example, I am looking at doing more work in Asia. To begin networking into the Asian market, I am joining and following Asia-focused groups and then begin participating in-group discussions. My goal is to find partnerships and help people understand who I am. When I see opportunities to help people in these networks, I am going to offer it up. I am going to help people in this new area as much as I can so when I need a favor or help with a project, I can float it out into my Asian network on LinkedIn and elsewhere.

Dirks: How can e-mail marketing and messaging help to cultivate and manage your personal brand within you network of contacts?

Van Yoder: This is the glue that holds everything together. We are in an information overload society. People are subscribing to more things online and getting more e-mails. You can only hold so much information in your mind at one time. So you cannot just have a great contact you met three years ago at a conference that hasn't heard from you since then and expect them to remember you when you need a job. The key is staying somewhat in touch with your contacts.

When you e-mail contacts, it must be professional and consistent with your personal brand. You want to be what we call in "top of mind" awareness within your network.

One way to do this is by sending out a newsletter. Businesses create newsletters to offer something of value back to customers and prospects. They stay in touch by offering something valuable. It is part of the giving philosophy behind Getting

Slightly Famous in action. So, you are doing two things at the same time.

If you do something like a newsletter you need to brand it. Give it a name and create a short and concise e-mail newsletter that you can blast to people you've met. Make sure your newsletter is focused and has no fluff. It could be a list of tips, resources, or opportunities in your industry or whatever information is relevant and helpful to those who read it. Be sure everyone who receives your newsletter wants to receive it and you are not spamming them.

In a job search you are reminding people about the good feelings that were generated when you met that person. You are showing in action, that you are a giver and thought leader in your industry. When you need to find job opportunities for advancing your career, you have a network that is ready, willing, and able to help you.

You should never think that the old rules of job search and advancing your career still apply. A lot of people take job security and career advancement for granted. They think they can be passive and not call attention to themselves. They think if they just show up, do a good job it will be good enough. This is not the case anymore. You have to be ruthlessly entrepreneurial and self-initiating about developing your personal brand. At the very least you will have a tremendous edge over most people who do not take this approach.

Becoming a Great Story Teller

One of the best ways to reinforce your personal brand is by demonstrating the value that it has. When you look back at your career, you should find more than a few accomplishments that you have produced, such as professional accomplishments that have overcome challenges and fixed business problems.

Before you get an interview for a potential position, you should have a series of career stories in your back pocket ready to go. Be careful not to fall into professional branding pitfalls, however. It is one thing to say you are the best at whatever you do. Everybody tries to play that game. It seems easy to say, "I am the best direct marketer you will find anywhere." To which any potential employer will say, "That is great, but prove it." It is the "proving it" part that gets people in trouble. If you cannot back up your personal brand, then your personal brand will suffer greatly. The gap between your brand statement (what value you provide to an employer) and the reality of what you actually did can create a wide credibility gap that is tough to overcome.

What many people have difficulty doing is being able to offer what we call in sales a "proof source." A proof source is a genuine and factual professional situation that you directly or indirectly had a hand in producing. If you want to have a compelling personal brand, you must be able to back it up with evidence that you can deliver on your brand.

The Three Skills of Story Telling

There are three basic skills included in telling your brand stories. The first skill is being able to concisely describe the challenge you faced. This could be anything you encountered along the road to your career experience. You should be able to clearly articulate what the parameters of your challenge were.

Example of describing the challenge:

"In July of last year, I was asked to take over a new product introduction team that had fallen well behind schedule. The challenge for me and the team was to deliver the new product by the original delivery date. We had severe time and budget constraints to overcome in order to deliver the expected results. The project was already three months behind schedule and was within 20 percent of its budget maximum for the project."

The next skill is being able to describe the actions you specifically took and provide a quick summary of why you took these actions. Focus on the critical actions you took without getting bogged down in the murkier details.

Example of describing your actions:

"After a few meetings with the team, it became apparent that several team members did not want to be on the team. I decided to work through that issue first as the motivation level of those who really wanted to participate was being negatively affected. We moved a few people back into their line positions and recruited some fresh and positive talent to the team to replace them."

The last skill is being able to share the results of your actions. This is the part where you are able make an impact by telling a brand story that leads up to a compelling end. Include answers to the following questions:

- What did you accomplish?
- Why was it so critical?
- What impact did this accomplishment have on the organization?
- What did it mean for you?

Being able to describe your professional experiences in a way that 1) captures the interest of your audience and 2) demonstrates you can back up your personal brand with bonafide experiences results in a successful story.

Your Marketing Collateral: Reinforcing Your Personal Brand

Marketing collateral is nothing more than printed or digital messaging in one form or another. A marketing or sales brochure is a basic form of collateral. It only serves to introduce you and/or reinforce your brand message. Any marketer worth his salt will tell you that any marketing or sales collateral created will not sell anything by itself.

There are a few collateral items that should be considered as a part of your personal branding strategy and creating differentiation between yourself and your job seeking competitors. This is not an exhaustive list by any means. Call it a basic list of collateral items you could produce or have professionally produced. Some items do not require much skill at all to implement. The point is clear: You need to leverage your personal branch message as much as possible in your job search campaign.

Business Cards and Letterhead

Having a set of your own professional "calling cards" that contains your basic contact information is key, especially if you have been laid off and are in the job search phase. This is one thing I highly recommend you create and use early in your search. How can you go to a networking event if you do not have a card? You cannot use your business card from your previous employer. Having a professionally-printed business card is the way to go.

Here are some quick guidelines for a personal but professional business card and letterhead:

1. Do not overload it with too much information. Keep it simple. Name, e-mail, phone, and mailing address are the basics. If you have a personal Web site or you want to print your LinkedIn or Facebook address, fine. Just do not feel obligated to fill every bit of white space on the card with data.

2. Avoid shocking colors or colors at all. It is tempting to differentiate yourself with a card that seems to stand out because of its design, but avoid the temptation. Keep the design to black print on a white background. Keep it simple and clean.

3. Avoid using exotic fonts. Like colors, exotic fonts can be hard to read and make a card and letterhead look even worse (and cheap). Have your printer recommend a font and a good size so that your card

reads easily. Do not agonize forever about how creative you can get with this piece of collateral.

4. Always have your cards and letterhead professionally printed on a high quality paper stock. Do not cheap out on thin, cheap paper for a card or letterhead.

5. Have a professional graphic designer provide you with multiple layouts that you can choose from. Unless you are a designer, you should not create your own layout. Rather, invest a few dollars into your marketing collateral to look crisp and professional.

E-mail Signatures

During your job search, you will use your e-mail accounts (for those of you like me who have multiple accounts for different reasons) hundreds of times, if not thousands of times per month. What a great opportunity to reinforce your brand each and every time you send out an e-mail. This is an opportunity not to be taken too lightly, either. The "tag line" you use says quite a bit about who you are and what you stand for. The truth is, most people either forget or ignore the fact that they have an opportunity to reinforce their personal brand by adding a few choice words and data at the end of every e-mail.

Here are some ways to make sure you are leveraging your e-mail signature every time you use it.

1. First, an important note on e-mail addresses. Keep your e-mail address crisp, clean, and simple. If you can reinforce a bit of your personal brand in it, fine. Just do not go too over board here. When you see an e-mail that is constructed as, crazyguy4u@company.com, such an e-mail does not come across as professional. Other names, such as sallyjohnsonbainesmith@company.com, can be a mouthful. Do your best to construct an e-mail name that is easy to remember.

Example:

smithmarketing@e-mail.com

You can construct an e-mail address to be relatively easy to re-member by simply marrying your name to the word "marketing" to make an attempt to remind people that you are a marketer (or what-ever your career is). Avoid slang names. Make your e-mail address easy to understand and remember.

2. An e-mail signature is designed to save you the time of have write a closing. Be sure your signature already incorporates your clos-ing and your name, preferably your full name. Do not, repeat, do not use your slang or nickname. Keep it professional at all times.

3. Pay attention to those who actually provide an e-mail signa-ture and find a style that seems to work best for you.

4. At a minimum, your e-mail signature should contain your clos-ing (Best, Dave); a tag line; your Web addresses (such as your personal Web site, blog, etc.); and your contact information.

If you want to add your mailing address to your signature, it is en-tirely up to you. For privacy and security purposes, I use my P.O. Box address on my e-mails when I do provide it. The annual cost of renting a box is a true business expense and worth the small price I pay to rent it.

Content Marketing

There is no better way to demonstrate your expertise than by developing and showcasing content that is proof of it. In a market-ing context, businesses of all shapes and sizes supply content in order to open lines of communication between themselves and potential customers. A newsletter, white paper, simple blog, or podcast are all examples of content marketing. Within your job search, you should create simple but effective content marketing that is tailored to spe-cific groups within your contact/network database.

During a job search, content marketing allows you to share your knowledge in ways that will be seen as helpful and value-added by the people you know. It is also designed to demonstrate what kinds of expertise you have and what kind of "thought leader" you really are.

A *thought leader* is someone who is on the cutting edge of his career field. He is the person who proactively shares his knowledge and insights as well as engages his peers in discussions both online and offline. A thought leader in any field usually stands out from his peers and has the industry/career stature that makes people want to listen to what he has to say.

Developing a Newsletter

If you consider yourself as a subject matter expert (everyone is an expert in something), then you might consider adding a professional newsletter to reinforce your personal brand. It is an excellent and inexpensive marketing tactic that can speak volumes about who you are and what you know.

During your job search, increase your exposure by creating a simple one- or two-page newsletter that shares some of that valuable information with the masses. A newsletter that is designed to showcase your expertise leverages your knowledge base beyond what your résumé will ever do for you. Look at the newsletter as a tool that helps you bolster your personal brand.

So how does this idea of producing your own professional newsletter come together? Here's how:

1. If you decide to create and produce your own newsletter, make sure you are committed to producing and distributing it on a regular and consistent basis. Creating a bimonthly newsletter only once is a waste of your time and will yield no results.

2. Use an electronic format for distributing your newsletter. Avoid the expense of having it printed and go with e-mail distribution. Creating a simple PDF file that can be attached to your e-mail is ideal. You can also think about having the newsletter laid into your e-mail.

3. Like all of the marketing collateral you will create during your job search campaign, make sure your newsletter looks professionally laid out. There is a lot of good software out there that can make that job easier if you insist being a designer yourself.

Apple's Pages software is very easy to use and comes with many professionally designed newsletter templates that can be modified if needed. It is worth the expense of having someone design a layout that you can use on your PC. For each issue, you simply delete the old copy and add the new copy.

4. Keep your newsletter to no more than one or two pages. You do not want to create a piece of job search collateral that takes up so much time to create that you lose valuable time doing other critical tasks.

5. Keep the name of your newsletter simple and clean. For example, a carpenter might have Insights on Woodworking or Budget Woodworking, etc. Do not agonize over this but be sure the title of your newsletter is connected to what it discusses. Be sure to have your name right below the title and formatted, such as Written by Susan Smith.

6. Content is king. If you are going to share your knowledge, make sure you really do that. This kind of newsletter should be positioned as valuable and helpful to those who might be interested in reading it. Remember your audience. You are trying to attract attention to recruiters and businesses in general.

Be sure the information you share about your knowledge and your accomplishments is clear and concise. After reading something, you audience should connect with it. Do not be cryptic and short on facts either. Create copy that helps people solve common problems faced in your industry.

Keep your newsletter to one or two pages and invest in writing copy that will be seen as insightful by recruiters, potential hiring managers, and potential referrals sources.

7. Proofread the copy carefully and have a few colleagues look it over, too. It does not hurt to have a friend or business colleague look it over to ensure spelling and grammar are tight and correct. Also, look for input from those whose opinions you trust for ideas or suggestions on making your content better.

8. Set up a regular publishing schedule. You do not need to publish monthly to be effective. However, I recommend a schedule of bi-monthly or at least quarterly to keep the momentum going and keep the newsletter collateral fresh.

9. Once you have your newsletter ready for distribution, attach it to every e-mail you send out. Place it on your blog and/or personal Web site. When you send your résumé out, make sure you add the newsletter as an attachment.

A professional newsletter will yield little if it is not used and/or it looks less than professional. It may not be a tactic for everyone, but a well designed and written newsletter is additional job search fire-power. It is also a great way to differentiate yourself from your competition.

Your Personal Web Site

To reinforce your personal brand and help generate some interest, you should consider creating your own personal job search-oriented Web site. The fact that you are in a job search mode should not be kept a secret. Having a professional Web-presence is insurance that you have resources working for your job search cause on a 24/7 basis.

Here are some tips to make sure you get the most mileage from your personal Web site for your job search campaign:

1. Use a Web address that is easy to remember and makes sense. The Web site used to promote this job search marketing book is www.jobsearchmarketing.net. My personal Web site for my outdoor writing is www.dirksoutdoors.com. It easily links my last name to what the focus and purpose of the Web site is. If you were an engineer you might use www.smithengineering.com to make the same point and reinforce your personal brand and name recognition.

2. Be sure your Web site looks professional, crisp, and clean. Unless you are a Web designer, do not attempt to do this on your own. Hire someone to do this if you can. If you cannot, find a software program similar to Apple's iWeb software that makes designing a professional looking Web site pretty easy to do.

Like anything else in life, first impressions are important, so be sure you have a well designed Web site. A messy and jumbled site will work against you and could deter your audience.

If you publish a photo of yourself, make sure the photo was taken by a professional photographer in a studio. Avoid trusting an amateur with this job, as you will pay the price.

3. Keep your Web site focused on one thing: showcasing who you are professionally and how you can be contacted. Keep your personal life out of this site if at all possible. Have your current résumé posted there and include anything else that will help a recruiter or employer get a sense of what your personal brand is all about.

4. Limit yourself to only a few pages of content. There is no need to make this an elaborate site. You might have an About Me page, which gives some professional information about you, including your résumé; another page dedicated to showcasing key accomplishments; and another page could contain your newsletter.

5. Keep your content fresh. Probably the number one killer of any Web site is a static site that never changes. If you use a personally branded Web site, commit to updating and refreshing your content on a weekly basis. Updates can be minor. Pick a page and find something to replace or update with new content. If you cannot update content weekly, then doing so at least monthly is an absolute minimum. Your résumé info does not need to change, but what you highlight about your knowledge and capabilities should.

6. Do not disclose too much personal information. Identity theft seems to increase everyday. For contact purposes, use e-mail as the primary point of contact. You can also list a phone number for direct contact as well. Leave out any references to your home mailing address. Be sure your résumé page blocks out your street address information and any other not necessary personal data. Regardless, make it easy for someone to contact you directly.

7. A personal Web site cannot single-handedly build your personal brand. A well-designed Web site helps you sell what you know and what you can do with what you know. A personal Web site can only reinforce your brand.

8. Do not expect your Web site to do the work for you. Its mission is not to qualify you for a job. Your personal Web site should only generate interest and point someone in your direction. In other words, your personal Web site is a contact point to direct interest and job leads you way. Even if it does not directly generate job leads, it reinforces your personal brand. Look at your Web site as just another distribution channel for getting your name and brand out.

9. When your Web site is up and running, let everyone know about it. You need to take responsibility in letting the world know that your Web site exists. E-mail friends, family, and business contacts. Tell them about your site's purpose in your job search. Be sure the Web address is printed on your business card, stationary, e-mail signature, and your résumé.

10. If you can, offer free items to elicit a response from those reviewing your site. If you publish a newsletter, be sure your recipients can easily request the latest edition for free. At a minimum, post newsletters, white papers, and other personally branded collateral on your site. This is your chance to show off what you know.

11. Be sure you can track and measure how many people visit your site and what pages they navigate to. It is important to have some way to measure your success in promoting the site. If you want to see a great example of a personal Web site, take a look at personal branding guru Dan Schawbel's Web site at www.danschawbel.com

Put Your Web Site to Work

Web site marketing leads to the creation of a flood of new Web sites every day. Yet, you will find few sites that are truly effective at either making money or increasing market visibility. A high-performing site is the exception, not the rule.

There is no better way to see the potential in your site than to dissect one that actually makes money and creates business opportunities. For our case study, we will use www.ducttapemarketing. com. Creator John Jantsch not only has a well thought out site, but he makes his living off of it. A well-known marketing consultant to small business, Jantsch has created a site that has all the right moving parts. His Web site is at www.ducttapemarketing.com. What does Jantsch do that most other Web sites do not?

• He offers tons of free advice related to the cause of helping you market your business better. He practices the marketing adage of "give and you will receive." Through his articles and blog tabs, you will find several books' worth of solid, practical advice and ideas, all for free. Why? Jantsch knows that he needs to give people a compelling reason to come back. And they do.

- He is creating a social community. The Internet has created an almost unlimited number of social networks that bring people with similar interests together. Jantsch knows that creating a place where people can share ideas by posting podcasts, videos, etc., makes his site a compelling place to be.

- He is not afraid to sell his wares throughout the site. The free and excellent content he gives away on the site whets the appetite for more content, which he is happy to sell you.

- He maintains an active blog on his site. A blog is a way to have a conversation on the Web. Jantsch posts fresh blog material just about every day. His readers react and share their thoughts, whether they agree with him or not. His blog is a place where he can test and develop new concepts or share some great resource that his readers crave.

- He links extensively with related sites. He is not bashful about introducing you to other sites that you can benefit from. Likewise, those sites also link back to his site. It is a reciprocal arrangement that he constantly looks to expand.

His Web site's parts add up to a compelling whole. Jantsch has created a site that has all the elements that allow him to make money and create more business opportunities. What's your Web site doing?

Blogging

Not too many years ago, the word "blog" or "blogging" would have mystified most people. The good news is that blogs and the process of blogging have grown exponentially in the last few years with millions of blogs now posted.

A blog is simply an online journal. Think of it as a way to express yourself in the Internet. The great thing about a blog is that it looks quite a bit like a personal Web site (you can also have a blog built into your personal Web site). With easy access to really exceptional blogging tools, such as Blogger and WordPress, you can have your own personal blog up and running in minutes.

In the context of a job search, having a blog is essential. Search engines love to crawl through public blogs. What better way to share your professional thoughts, insights, and experiences with the world with an online journal?

Today, you will hear a lot about "thought leadership." Being a thought leader means that you have the knowledge and experience to share valuable information with an audience that is interested in what you do or say. A well designed and frequently updated blog can go a long way to increasing your brand exposure, as well as enhancing your brand at the same time. For a job search, it is a beautiful thing.

Here are a few ideas to keep your blog focused as a personal branding and job search tool.

1. Like a personal Web site, make sure you have a blog address that makes sense and helps your brand. My blog is www.growingmy-business.wordpress.com. I did not design it for a job search but it has the same impact because it allows me to share my thoughts on marketing to a world audience. If I was in a job search, I might have created www.dirksmarketing.wordpress.com. You also have the option of having a blog built right into your personal Web site, which is the ideal strategy.

2. The only cost to you for starting a blog is your time. Using a blog builder site, such as WordPress or Blogger, you can access excellent and free tools to set up your blog.

3. Be sure anyone who reads your blog understand that you are in a job search. Have a tab or section on your blog that stands out and has information about you availability for hire. Do not keep this a secret. Make it known and clear. Have all your contact information easily notable and accessed.

- 160 -

4. Once you have your blog up and running, you need to immediately and continually let people know about it. Send out an electronic press release to all your e-mail list members including friends, relatives, business contacts, and any recruiters. Encourage all of your contacts to share that information with their friends. If you can get your contact list to forward your e-mail announcing your blog to their e-mail lists, you will give yourself a healthy and fast start to growing your initial blog audience.

Be sure you send a press release to all the local media that describes your blog and the types of things you will be discussing and sharing within it. The media is always on the prowl for a good story, so make sure you give them a good angle that gets their attention.

With an RSS feed, your blogging audience can ensure they know when you have provided a new post on your blog. An RSS (which stands for Rich Site Summary) is a mechanism that allows you to aggregate feeds from different sources (news blogs and websites where you can sign up to receive information that can be sent to your e-mail address for example). The RSS feed alerts your readers via e-mail when that happens. However, do not rely on that alone. When you have a special update, it will not hurt to alert your e-mail list from time to time. Do not send out an alert e-mail to your contact list every time you update your blog. E-mailing your contact list too often tires out your audience and eventually they will tune you out.

Be sure you have your blog address located on your e-mail signature (along with you personal Web site address if you use one as well).

5. Write meaty and well-written posts. Whatever your expertise, remember your audience is looking for honest and insightful perspectives from you. It does not matter what profession or trade you are in, just be sure you make your posts informative and interesting to your specific audience to make them want to come back to your blog again and again.

The topics you can cover on a blog are fairly wide but I would stay within the context of your job search campaign and focus only on your area of expertise. If you are a horticulturalist, for example, you can cover a wide range of issues related to the horticulture industry and your own expertise.

Same thing would apply for a political campaign manager, electrical engineer, or landscaper. There is always something going on in your field and a blog is a good way to discipline yourself to stay abreast of happenings in your area of expertise.

6. Keep your blog open and allow your audience to comment on your postings. As you develop and grow your blogging audience, you will begin to see others start to respond to your postings. Your timely response encourages a wider and sometimes deeper discussion about a certain topic. You can expect to see a lot of spam but both WordPress and blogger have very good anti-spam programs to police this issue.

7. Never post anything bad about any previous employer you have had. Never post information that is too personal in nature. Employ common sense in what you decide to post.

8. Post regularly. This is one of the biggest mistakes that many bloggers make right out of the gate. During your job search campaign (and beyond), put yourself on a regular schedule for posting blogs. While the frequency is entirely up to you, I recommend posting no less than once per week and more frequently if you can.

9. Contribute to other select blogs and be sure to insert an inbound link to your blog to help increase your exposure during your job search campaign.

Social Media Marketing Best Practices by Leap Frog Interactive
Provided with permission from www.leapfroginteractive.com

- It is important to be honest and engaging in social media (like blogs). Users will quickly identify those marketing activities that are disingenuous.
- Be sure to keep adding fresh material. New content, consistently posted will provide a reason for your contacts to remain engaged. This involvement also helps support the sincerity mentioned above.
- Share interesting links and news related to your industry. Linking will improve the chances of other online users discovering the brand.
- Be sure to provide tagging on your blog postings to help search engines and readers know what the post is about.
- Be sure the titles of the blog postings are interesting and can grab the interest of the readers and get them to read your content.
- Be visual. Using pictures can help convey your point of view and also be funny and informative in its own right.
- It is important that you check spelling and grammar in its social media content.
- You need to monitor user comments for overly abusive ones and remove them accordingly.
- Respond to criticism and concerns with honest and sincere regard.
- Once involved, stay involved. Abandoned conversation can hold a negative impact for brands (meaning your personal brand).

Podcasting

Another way to integrate and expand your personal brand during a job search is to create and post podcasts. A podcast is simply an audio version of a blog. iTunes is a great place to see just how important podcasting has become for all sorts of business brands. There you will see a wide range of topics covered by both corporations and individuals. A simple but well-engineered podcast is like having your own radio show.

Here are a few key points when considering podcasting:

1. Think of a podcast as an extension of your personal Web site and blog. Integrating the look, feel, and content of your podcast to align with your other job search marketing efforts is critical to long-term success in this arena. One of the ways to accomplish this is using a current topic from your blog to create a more extensive discussion using an audio podcast.

2. For the non-technical, podcasting should not scare you. There are great programs out there that are designed to be easy for just about anyone (including me and you) to record and edit a podcast so that it sounds professional. If you want to go the free software route, you can download Audacity to your Mac or PC and start recording right from there.

You may also have a friend or business contact that has already taken the plunge and has podcasting experience. It is wise to consult with these friends, too.

3. Like anything else you produce, make sure you produce content that is worth listening to. Like your personal Web site, blog, and newsletter, your podcast has to offer your listening audience something worth the time to download the MP3 file of your podcast.

4. Organization is important when podcasting. Unless you feel extremely comfortable with the material you want to cover during the podcast, always make a general outline of the topics you want to cover and their natural sequence. I can discuss almost any marketing topic right off the top of my head, but I still use an outline to keep me focused and on track.

5. Keep your podcasts concise and short. There are plenty of podcasts you can find that can go sixty minutes or longer. My suggestion is to record them in the two minute to fifteen minute range. Many people have the attention span of a gnat these days, so being

concise and delivering you information within a few minutes is key. Do not drone and stick to your outline. From time to time you may need more than fifteen minutes to get your points out, but try to stay within fifteen minutes or less as much as possible.

6. Once again, let everyone you know in on your new podcasts. Whether you offer them on your Web site and other sites (like iTunes), you need to make sure everyone knows about it. Be sure to note it on your e-mail signatures, too.

7. Most importantly, podcast on a regular basis. Like blogging, you need to put yourself on a schedule of providing podcasts that works for you. Do not overload yourself by saying you will podcast everyday because the truth is, you will not. Create a realistic schedule that is coordinated with other content sources you produce during your job search campaign like your Web site, blog, newsletters, and e-mail updates.

Vodcasting

Another excellent opportunity to expand your brand and extend your reach during your job search is by producing vodcasts. Vodcasting is just an extension of podcasting but done in video format. With each passing year, basic video equipment and editing software offer great product quality and features with lower and lower prices. Armed with a video camera and some basic software (like Apple's iMovie), you, too, can produce quality video that can be displayed almost anywhere.

With the advent of YouTube and other places to aggregate video content, a whole new world has opened up in the context of a job search campaign. If a vodcast is done well, it can go a long way towards extending your brand and reach. However, nothing will bring your personal brand down faster than a poorly produced vodcast.

With that in mind, here are few key points to keep in mind with respect to vodcasting:

1. Walk before you run. The video cameras made today and the editing software are easy enough to use. The challenge is to make sure you have some experience preparing, shooting, editing, and uploading your vodcasts. The good news is that you can shoot as many practice vodcasts as you need to get comfortable with the technology and reduce your anxiety about using it.

2. Organization is a must, not an option. Try to fly from the seat of your pants while doing a video and you will soon learn a painful lesson. Do that and you will simply look silly, unprofessional and do more harm than good to your personal brand. There are plenty of excellent materials available to help you produce a quality video.

3. Keep vodcasts short in duration within range of between one to ten minutes maximum. Nobody has the time to listen to a sixty-minute diatribe on whatever topic. Keep the vodcast focused and to the point.

4. Be sure you compress the completed vodcast into a format that makes it as small as possible but retains a decent level of playback quality. Next to poor quality, the worst thing you can do is create a vodcast that takes too long to download.

5. Look the part in order to enhance your personal brand. In other words, look and act on camera within the context of the profession you are in. If you are in the medical profession, you might wear a lab coat when you are on camera. Wear the appropriate uniform of your profession. Never forget that you are conducting a job search campaign and your next employer may be checking you out.

6. Content is king, and be sure your content on a vodcast is interesting and valuable to those who are going to see it.

7. Like blogging, podcasting, or an e-newsletter, it's critical to schedule and produce vodcasts on a regular basis. You determine the schedule but make it frequent enough so that you create some buzz around your vodcasts, keep the content fresh, and give your audience a reason to come back for more.

8. Be sure everyone knows that you are providing vodcasts within your contact list. Add the address where people can find your vodcasts (i.e., iTunes, blog, and Web site). Be sure you have it noted in your e-mail signature, too. Have you heard this stuff before? It is always worth repeating that if you do not market it, they will not come.

YouTube 101

Increasingly, business owners, industry experts, and job seekers are finding out that a short, ten minute or less video posted on You-Tube can open the world to them and their expertise. It is a completely inexpensive way to display some of your expertise to the world. Here are a few ideas of things to talk about on a YouTube video for all kinds of businesses:

Accountant: Ten-Year End Tax Tips
Example: http://www.youtube.com/watch?v=m_210yr0ryQ

Chef: How to Make Chicken Marsala
Example: http://www.youtube.com/watch?v=JgaeuC4OsGQ
Author/Publisher: How to Write a Book
Example: http://www.youtube.com/watch?v=yXMghQTGNLs

Fishing Tackle dealer: How to Use a Flasher to Improve Your Fishing
Example: http://www.youtube.com/watch?v=DRk-RnZStyl

To make your posting effective, you will have to promote the location of your YouTube videos in all of your sales, marketing, and networking efforts. Make sure you reference them in your e-mails, flyers, brochures, and even your business card. Do your part to be sure locals can find your video postings. Be sure you direct YouTube visitors back to your Web site. YouTube is a free way to get additional exposure for you and your expertise.

Publish or Perish

We can learn a thing or two from what is almost a standard procedure at most large and influential universities in the world. Professors are required to publish research papers and studies on a regular basis. Universities require this kind of extra effort, in addition to their academic/student responsibilities, because it helps to drive knowledge innovation and build the corporate brand of the university. Publishing also helps to boost the brand reputation of any professor. Publishing and conducting research also keeps professors sharp and on the cutting edge of their knowledge base.

Publishing white papers (authoritative reports that address problems and how to solve them) on your own is another way to increase and deepen your brand exposure. Your completed white papers and other commentaries should be posted on your personal Web site and blog. If you want to demonstrate your creativity and intellectual power and expertise, there is no better way than by writing and publishing your own papers.

Here are a few guidelines that are worth mentioning:

1. Have a professional graphic designer create a simple and nicely designed format that you can use to lay your copy into. Nothing speaks louder than a professional and sharp looking layout. Include a title page, content page (which you can then use to add more or less pages) and the last page, which should be fully dedicated to providing the reader information about you. Make it clear that you are seeking employment opportunities by just saying so in your overview or introduction section.

The bio page should give the reader a short one- or two-paragraph biography of yourself and your contact information. Contact information should at least include your Web site address, blog address (if applicable), e-mail address, and a reliable phone number.

2. Keep your reports, white papers, and other research concise. No need to write a tome on any particular subject. Keep it focused on just the meat and potatoes. Keep it to no more than ten pages maximum if you can.

3. Write about key issues or events that are important to your reading audience. You should write about key issues or challenges facing your industry as much as possible. You do not have to solve world problems, but it does not hurt to expose your professional opinion on a hot topic.

4. Stay away from being controversial or divisive. Unless you are a political consultant, stay away from lightening rod issues that are politically charged. Stay focused on writing about the things in your industry that are worth discussing and vetting ideas. You want to publish papers that are insightful and helpful to those who are reading them. Leave the controversial positions at home.

5. A poorly published paper can devastate your personal brand almost overnight. Have your writing proofread and copyedited before publishing it.

6. Promote, promote, and promote! It does you no good to invest time writing white papers if know one knows about it. Post your papers on your Web site, blog, and promote them using your e-mail signature. You might even send a copy along with a press release to your local newspaper editors and include other local media, such as local television and radio. All media outlets need fresh new material and story ideas every day, 24/7. You might just write a white paper that finds you getting an interview on the morning or evening news.

Going Long: Writing a Book

There may not be a better way to promote your personal brand than to share it with the world by writing a book. Some might have reservations about writing a book, simply because it is a big undertaking. In most cases, you can self-publish your book without spending a fortune on it. As a matter of fact, with print-on-demand publishing capabilities today, almost anyone can publish a book. I suggest you look at POD publishers, such as BookSurge (www.booksurge.com).

Let's get one thing clear here: writing a book is not easy at all. It is not for everyone, and it is not a deal killer if you are not interested in writing one. Writing a book is not a must do, but it comes "highly recommended" by me. It takes a commitment of time and intellectual capital from you.

The rewards for the effort you make to publish your expertise are excellent. A book that shares your expertise is a market differentiator. If you are looking for a way to survive in the long run and create some separation from you and your competition, write and publish a book.

Herbalist/Author Gene Ladd is a good friend of mine who spent years in herbal healthcare business. To expand his personal brand and reach, he wrote two books that he sells at an amazing profit margin; he is well-recognized locally and regionally for his expertise. He promotes his business and his expertise everywhere he goes. It clearly separates him from the crowd.

Often people will feel limited by their writing skills. Do not let that deter you. If you want to do it bad enough, you will find someone who will help. There are many tools available to you—as well as freelance writers and editors—who can help you in the writing process.

Differentiate yourself from the crowd by sharing and selling your expertise in the form of a book.

Adding Viral Marketing to Your Job Search Campaign

Viral marketing can give you an edge in a crowded market where building awareness is difficult and sometimes downright expensive from a marketing point of view. Viral marketing is defined as creating word-of-mouth campaigns that can help you establish market differentiation. Market differentiation is the ability to stand out from your competitors as a leader in the market.

Viral marketing can also be defined as the process of getting groups of people to spread the word about your business or whatever you want to showcase by word of mouth or e-mail. Using biological terms, you infect a small group of people who influence other people to check you out. One person tells two, those two people tell other people, and so the process rolls on. It is a kind of marketing that has people spreading the word about you for free. It is the "free" part of viral marketing that makes it so attractive to folks who hear about it.

It is important to note that viral marketing is not based on executing just one campaign. Rather, it is based on the ability to create several different "viral'" tactics and launching them on an ongoing basis throughout the year.

Here are some ideas for creating viral marketing campaigns:

1. Write and publish a series of free e-books utilizing your expertise in ways that help potential customers learn valuable lessons. E-books (e for electronic) should be well-designed, brief, and available in a downloadable PDF file. If you have expertise, then you should consider writing a series of e-books that handle specific topics that would be of interest to current and potential customers.

E-books are not sales presentations. They should be full of meaty information that helps people do or manage something better. They are an opportunity to showcase your expertise and talent.

2. Create a short video that can be downloaded from your own site as well as sites, such as YouTube. In a video clip that should be less than two minutes long, offer viewers an opportunity to learn from

you. Be sure that you promote these videos heavily. Get the word out to friends, family, and contacts, and remember that it takes time to build an audience. Create a regular stream of new videos on a regular basis and you will see interest start to expand. People will see your videos and pass the links on to others they know.

3. Create a blog that allows you to showcase your expertise and create a dialogue with current and potential clients.

When I started my blog in early 2007, www.growingmybusiness. wordpress.com, we had only a few followers. Now, I have hundreds of readers and my base grows exponentially each month. A blog is a great way to create some viral marketing and spread the word about you and your expertise.

Expert Insights with David Meerman Scott

David Meerman Scott is the bestselling author of The New Rules of Marketing & PR and the new hit book World Wide Rave and one of the foremost experts in the of viral marketing. Check out his blog at www.webinknow.com and his Website: www.davidmeermanscott. com.

Dirks: In the context of conducting a job search, why should someone consider viral marketing as a part of a job search strategy?

Meerman Scott: You want to find a new job? You have to stop thinking like an advertiser of a product and start thinking like a publisher of information.

Create information that people want. Create an online presence that people are eager to consume. Establish a virtual front door that people will happily link to. And one that employers will find.

As I have said at every speech I give, "On the Web, you are what you publish." It is no different when the product is you, and you are looking for a job.

Dirks: What are some ways that viral marketing can be integrated into the job search process?

Meerman Scott: You want people to talk about you. You want communities of people who eagerly link to your stuff on the Web. You want online buzz to drive buyers to your virtual doorstep.

There are many ways to get out there into the social media world. Start a blog that highlights your expertise. Create a Twitter feed. Shoot some videos. Establish a podcast channel where you interview people in your industry. Write an e-book that dives deep into a subject you know. Comment on the blogs and in the forums and chat rooms that are important to the business of prospective employers.

The new rules of finding a job require you to share your knowledge and expertise with a world that is looking for what you have to offer.

Dirks: How can viral marketing as a concept help the job seeker to differentiate himself in a very competitive job market?
Meerman Scott: I am on the board of directors of several companies. When looking at candidates for a job, which do you think gets more attention from board members: A résumé? Or a well-written blog or e-book?

If you follow this strategy to find a new job, an added benefit is that you will stay in the mix. You will not get stale. Instead of sending out résumés all day and trudging to "informational interviews" where you *tell* people what you can do, you will publish things that *show* them that you would be a smart addition to the team. You will stay fresh and connected to your marketplace.

Dirks: What are five common mistakes you see most people make when it comes to using viral marketing to increase their personal brand and differentiating themselves?

Meerman Scott: What comes up when you Google your name with the name of your most recent employer? Potential employers do that all the time. And you can influence what they see! Remember, on the Web you are what you publish.

The biggest mistake is that some people think they are sellers of a product (that is what a résumé does). Instead, they must think along the lines of a publisher of interesting information that their buyers (companies that may want to hire you) will want to consume. Remember that people are looking for you.

Some people might argue that this technique only works to find jobs related to social media and online marketing. Not true. I am convinced that this technique works for many other kinds of roles, too. And here is an added benefit: If you are an accountant, or salesperson, or production manager looking for work via social media, you really are going to stand out from the crowd.

Dirks: Any other comments/suggestions that you would have for the person who is undertaking a job search campaign in the context of leveraging viral marketing in his search strategy?

Meerman Scott: Yes, it is tough to find a new gig. I have been there. Three times. But it is a heck of a lot easier if you put yourself out there and generate the sort of information that employers will find valuable in an employee.

Expand your Reach with Audio Marketing

Audio marketing is a great way to attract attention and build personal brand recognition. It is also a very cost-effective way to market your expertise and products, and it is cost-effective to do so from the convenience of your home. Since people can call in from any location around the country, audio marketing also gives you geographic reach you cannot always get from other marketing campaign alternatives.

Here are a few easy steps to get you started on the path to audio marketing success in your job search campaign:

1. Find a cost-effective conference call vendor. Use a vendor that can provide reliable audio conferencing services that allow you to record the calls for audio playback that you can then place on your Web site or blog. Being able to offer the recorded sessions on different media such as Web site and CDs increases your effectiveness and reach. Try www.freeconferencepro.com, which offers exceptional audio conferencing services for free; it provides a service that would cost extra from other hosting services.

2. Find topics that can help customers solve critical problems. Create audio conferences that offer plenty of information. Pick topics that you know would be considered high-value topics to your customer base. Invite other industry experts to join you to discuss specific subjects.

3. Develop a regular flow of calls, and stick with it. The worst you can do is just doing one or two calls and then stop. That is a dead end for sure.

4. Keep the calls between thirty and sixty minutes. Like any presentation, your audio call should have a beginning (how will this call help listeners?); a middle (give them the juice and wow them with your solutions); and a close (how can we help?). Be sure to leave enough time for a question-and-answer session.

5. Promote, promote, promote. Every scheduled call you host should be broadcast to your entire contact/network database. Create a page on your personal Web site for a listing of upcoming Webinar's and other calls. Key hiring managers in your targeted organizations should be on top of the list. List it in every local publication you can think of.

6. Sell yourself. Every call you host is a new opportunity to showcase the depth of your expertise and product knowledge. By showing those on the call how you can help them solve real problems in their

lives or businesses, you extend the depth of your impact on them. You give them another reason to tune in and spend time with you.

7. Offer these calls for free. You are not in the business of selling the calls. You are in the business of creating a path for people to rely on you as an expert.

Paper, Ink, and Postage Stamps

Probably the most powerful way to build a strong personal brand is driven not by technology but rather by the power of paper, ink, and a postage stamp. It is "old school" personal brand building that never goes out of style. It is probably the simplicity of this technique and the fact that so few people actually do it that make this technique so powerful for branding.

The act of sending someone a handwritten note has a way of creating a branding moment that is usually remembered long after the note is lost or tossed out. When was the last time you received a personal, handwritten note as a thank you for something or as a follow-up to a meeting or event? If you have ever received a handwritten note from a business contact, you probably know how it feels to get it. More often than not, it changes for the better the way you perceive that person. It reinforces and builds on a positive characteristic that is essential to the personal brand.

More than anything, taking the time to handwrite a short note immediately impresses those on the receiving end. That is because so few people are willing to take the time to mail a handwritten note. Personalization in a mass-market world has always been a way to differentiate yourself from the crowd. The more you deploy this strategy, the more it enhances your personal brand.

In the context of conducting a job search and developing a strong personal brand, using handwritten notes is icing on the cake. The best news is that most of your competition does not.

Here are a few things to keep in mind when using the "handwritten notes" strategy:

1. The key to making handwritten notes effective is to do them on a regular and consistent basis. Here is where most people fall off. They will send handwritten notes for a time and then drop off and never find the time again. My suggestion is to find at least one person per day that you can send a note of congratulations, thank you, or a follow-up from a meeting or interview.

Anyone who helps you during your job search should get a handwritten note of thanks. Every recruiter who directly or indirectly helps you should get a handwritten note of thanks. Generally, anyone who you meet with on the phone, face-to-face, or during a Web-based event should get a note from you.

2. Invest in a good quality note card with matching envelopes. Incorporate the handwritten note strategy, and you will find the money you spend on note cards and postage will pay off many times.

3. If appropriate, attach a recent article or piece of information you know will be of interest to them. As you meet and network with people during your job search, you will get to know them better. And knowing them better means you will understand their interests, likes, and dislikes in both a personal and business context.

A handwritten note with a clip from a recent magazine article on a topic you know is of some importance to them can have a powerful effect. It is powerful in its ability to do two things for you: By helping your contact, 1) you deepen the relationship and earn some goodwill and 2) your personal brand gets an instant boost. You begin to develop a relationship for being thoughtful and helpful at the same time. There is no price you can put on that kind of brand reputation.

4. Keep the tone on the note warm but business-like. Unless you know them very well, it may be a bit of a stretch to come off too chummy. Keep your message simple and on point. If it is a thank you note,

then make sure the contacts understand fully why you are thanking them.

5. Do not become a "note stalker." Be sure you send notes to as many different people as possible. Sure, you might find yourself sending the same person more than one note, but do not do it every week. Spread your brand reputation around.

If all you did was deploy the strategy of crafting handwritten notes and nothing else to develop and bolster your personal brand, it would be enough. If done consistently, it is very powerful. Remember, many might think about doing this, but most rarely follow through and make it a habit.

Staying Current on Trends and Issues in Your Field

Whether you are in a job search or not, finding the time to keep current on the latest issues in your field can be trying. Top performers who have carefully crafted their personal brands are usually the same ones who make it a point to stay in the know on their area of expertise.

Being on the cutting edge of the latest issues of any career field is even more critical if you are conducting a job search. If you do not keep up on trends and news in your field, you will look like Web 0.0.

Here are some of key points to consider when trying to stay on top of news and trends in your field and areas of expertise:

1. Invest in online or hardcopy subscriptions to the leading magazines in your field. You need not subscribe to them all, but some investment on your part is more than prudent in light of the fact that you will be better positioned against your competition.

2. If you understand your areas of development (what you need to improve or strengthen), then you might also want to look into the opportunity to take workshops or courses for improvement. Look at continuing your education during a job search as a way to invest in yourself and to position your brand. At the very least, it is quite inex-

pensive to read the latest books on your career topics that could add to your education.

I once worked for a company that was winding down its operations after declaring bankruptcy. Several months before the business closed, I invested in some executive education and signed up for an excellent program at the University of Michigan's Ross School of Business.

Given that I was only months from an inevitable layoff, most people would have thought that spending $5,000 of my own hard-earned cash on a graduate level executive program would have been foolish. I felt very differently about it. Even though I was already in a senior level marketing position, I wanted to be sure I was on the cutting edge of market strategy and positioned well against any competitors I might face during my job search. Looking back, it was one of the best investments I have made in my career and I have since done it several times more…each time at my own expense.

3. This fact may seem obvious, but do not sign up for just any course that looks like it will help you fill out some areas of your personal brand. When shopping for some additional educational resources, check out as many as possible. It pays to really do your homework and understand what the program or course objectives are versus what you need in order to position yourself against your potential competition in the job market. My advice is to stick to well-known programs that have an existing reputation for providing high-quality educational programs, workshops, and seminars.

4. After you complete any program, make sure you have a way to let others know about your accomplishment. Remember, you are not only investing in your career, but you are also expanding your educational opportunities to strengthen your personal brand. Let the world know about it by sending a note to your e-mail contact list; posting it on your social networking pages (i.e., LinkedIn, Facebook, MySpace, etc.); or posting it on your Web site, blogs, etc.

Rick Bronder on Growing Your Knowledge & Skill Base

Rick Bronder has over thirty years experience in business, team development, long-range planning, coaching, management, and leadership development. He operates and owns a small but highly successful consulting practice, Possibility Plus. You can e-mail Rick at rbronder@gmail.com.

Want to become more effective or more efficient? High-performing people know how to do that. They use a three-pronged strategy for improving their knowledge and skills:

- Read a book a month on management or leadership.
- Listen to CDs or watch DVDs about management topics.
- Associate with successful people.

1. Read a book a month. Many insist they do not have the time to read a book a month. Once you make it a priority, you can accomplish this goal. If you cannot find the time to read a book a month, as an alternative, you could subscribe to an executive summary service. There are plenty out there. Start your search by typing "book summary service" into Google. Most of these companies will let you try their service for free. Try them until you find the one you like.

Once you get your summaries, be selective on what books you read. Here is a tip to help you decide if a book is worth finishing. When you get the book, place a bookmark at the halfway mark. Now, as you read the book, make notations on new things you are learning, especially new techniques you can use to improve your management ability.

If you reach the original bookmark and you do not have at least five entries in your log, do not finish the book. You can save a lot of time using this approach. Yes, you may miss some good suggestions, but you will get a high return on your time investment. Create a book club where you and others read a book and then share your thoughts on the book's merits.

2. Listen to CDs or watch DVDs about management topics. Use your commute time to listen to CDs, if possible. Try to focus on motivational speakers since it is not a good practice to take notes while driving!

Not all of your CDs need to be motivational. With CDs, you may need to listen to the speaker multiple times to get the message. Listening to motivational speakers can make a big difference in your effectiveness.

3. Associate with successful people. Is there an AMA (American Management Association) chapter near you? If yes, join and attend networking events. If there is no AMA, then look for local business associations that sponsor networking events. One of the best ways to make sure you are associating with successful people is to create your own group. Meet once a month or once a quarter to swap best practices in management.

Expert Insights with Rick Rochon: On Branding and Networking

Rick Rochon is a marketing specialist dedicated to educating and training small business owners to market smarter. Check out his blog at http://blog.rickrochon.com and his Web site at www.rickrochon.com

Dirks: In the context of conducting a job search, why should someone be concerned about developing and presenting their personal brand?

Rick Rochon: I think that our personal brand is an essential component of a job search. Who I am, what I stand for, and how I present myself is a direct reflection of my personal brand. It is how other humans connect with other humans. We all have a brand and our brand is how we establish meaningful connections with other people that connect with that brand. Although we often think of brands for large companies, in this context brand is about me and my persona, not necessarily me and my personality.

Dirks: There are so many Web sites/resources that offer social marketing opportunities today. How would you suggest a job seeker narrow down his choices of which social networks will be most effective for him (outside of job aggregators, such as HotJobs, Monster, etc.)?

Rochon: First, determine the best places to connect with professionals in your industry. I highly recommend LinkedIn for job searches. It gives the job seeker the ability to search for jobs via Indeed.com and see what connections in his network can assist him in getting into that company. Additionally, Jobster is a fantastic resource for socially marketing yourself as a potential employee to employers. From the recruitment side, there are some interesting companies, such as Jobvite, that facilitate the social relationship between companies and potential employees.

Dirks: What are five common mistakes you see people make when they try to engage social marketing to extend their marketing reach?

1. Not leveraging their knowledge and expertise.
2. Being a commercial for themselves and over promoting.
3. Sharing irrelevant information.
4. Sharing too much and inundating the fan or follower.
5. Having a monologue with their followers and not engaging in a conversation.

Dirks: Any other comments/suggestions that you would have for the person who is undertaking a job search campaign as it relates to leveraging social marketing?

Rochon: Social marketing and networking is the best way to get access to a group of people that can really "cut the curve" of your job search. Give back to those people, participate in your community, leverage yourself as the expert in your space, and great things will happen.

Freelance is the New Full-time

Another great strategy you can employ during a job search is to network yourself into freelance projects as an independent contractor. The advantages are two-fold: 1) you are going to expand your network of business contacts, especially in your area of expertise, so use the freelance opportunity as a way to break the ice and show off your expertise and value; and 2) it is also a great way to earn extra cash when you need it the most! Freelancing is truly an opportunity that you should evaluate and consider as a part of your job search marketing campaign. Also, it may work out to be a full-time business for you over time. You just never know until you try.

Here are a few guidelines when considering the freelancing component:

1. Freelancing can help you in your job search but only if you stick to selling your expertise. If you did your marketability assessment thoroughly and honestly, you should have a very definite idea of the specific services you can provide to your customers, whether they are businesses or individuals. You should be able to make a list of what services you can provide and provide a written, detailed description of what each entails.

2. Promote, promote, promote. If you decide to offer your freelance services, it is fairly easy to integrate and promote your services into your job search campaign. During networking, make sure you mention that you also offer freelance services in your area of expertise.

Your e-mail signature should contain a reference about your freelance services. For example, you could simply add the words "Need to make your marketing more effective? Ask me about my freelance services." If you have a Web site and/or blog, make sure you have a reference point for letting people know that you are available for freelance hire. Consider adding a page dedicated to your freelance services. Simply put, you should promote your freelance services at every opportunity.

3. Do not quit your day job of finding another job. Balance your time between your job search campaign and freelance activities. Until you start promoting your services, it is hard to estimate how much time that might eat out of your job search campaign time.

On one hand, freelance projects can generate needed income, showcase your expertise, and keep your skills sharp. On the other hand, you need to still dedicate time to implementing your job search campaign outside of freelancing. That balance between using free-lancing for networking and income generation and the need to at-tend to other critical parts of your job search campaign only becomes a challenge when you actually have freelance projects to do. It is a great problem to have.

4. How to organize your freelance business is not within the scope of this book. However, I suggest you consult with your accountant and attorney to get some input on what your options are for organizing your freelance business for income and tax purposes.

5. If you are able to obtain and complete freelance projects, make sure you note that on your various social networking platforms, such as Linkedin and Facebook. You do not have to note the name of the firm but it is a great way to let people know you are active and mov-ing yourself forward. Showcasing completed projects may also help you generate more interest from others who may need your services. Any freelance projects you take on should be part of your portfolio of completed work projects.

6. You might think about joining a professional organization that serves your field of expertise. Find out how they can help you ex-pand your network of contacts and help you find potential freelance projects. Joining a professional organization should be on your list of things to do regardless of whether you decide to freelance or not.

Expert Insights with Catherine Kaputa

Catherine is the author of the award-winning U R a Brand: How Smart People Brand Themselves for Business Success, winner of the Ben Franklin award for best career book 2007, a bronze medal in the IPPY awards, and a finalist for the 2007 Career Book of the Year award in Foreword magazine. Check out her Web site at www.self-brand.com.

Dirks: In the context of conducting a job search, why should someone be concerned about developing and presenting his personal brand?

Catherine Kaputa: It has probably never been harder to find a job than it is today. Not only do we face a poor economy with companies shedding jobs seemingly by the minute, but we also face global competitors for our jobs, since so many can be outsourced to cheaper labor markets around the world, even more sophisticated jobs that were thought to be immune.

That is where branding can help you stand out. When you think like a brand, you think of yourself as a "product" in a competitive marketplace, and create a "brand promise." A brand promise is your USP (Unique Selling Proposition) of what you stand for that is different, relevant, and adds value. Like a brand, you package yourself with a visual identity and verbal identity so that you consistently convey your brand promise or USP.

Dirks: What are some ways that personal branding can be integrated into the job search process and why?

Kaputa: First of all, use your résumé to tell a story about Brand You. Your résumé is often the first impression you make with an employer or business associate. And first impressions are important. That first minute read of your résumé decides whether your résumé gets pitched in the circular file, or whether you are perceived as a six-figure candidate who can add value to the organization and called in for an interview.

Your résumé also helps people position you and compare you to other candidates—and a great résumé can pre-sell you before you get the interview. That is why it is important that your résumé is a marketing document that tells your story in the best possible way and resonates in the current marketplace.

Here are some ideas for creating a winning résumé:

1) View your résumé as an "ad" for Brand You. Most résumés are a laundry list of skills and jobs written in "corporate speak" with no focus or message. Develop a single-minded positioning (your USP) that differentiates you from others and is relevant to the company and what is hot in the current job market. The résumé should tell the story of that positioning and link the various aspects of your career in a coherent whole.

2) Do not neglect graphic appeal. Keeping the ad analogy, make sure the résumé looks graphically appealing. Not only is the content dramatically different in a résumé that is an effective branding document, the layout and graphic design makes the résumé exciting and eye-catching.

3) Use a profile statement to position yourself and grab attention. Your profile at the top of your résumé is like the headline and lead paragraph in an ad. The profile should convey your brand promise: identify who you are, what sets you apart from others, and the value added that you bring to a job. A profile should not only differentiate you, it should convey a compelling reason to choose you and not the other people you are competing against. And it must say this in an arresting way.

Here is a typical example of a profile:

Proven sales professional with over twenty years experience. Team player with good interpersonal skills. Extensive experience in wide range of industries. Successfully managed regional sales force.
There are two key problems with this profile: One, it uses generalities and clichés we've seen before in hundreds of résumés.

Secondly, it does not differentiate this sales executive from other people with similar experience.

Here is a new profile:

*SALES LEADER * STRATEGIST * MOTIVATOR*

The salesperson's sales person who thrives in challenging markets and loves to negotiate the impossible. Capture business opportunities by doggedly pursuing new business and marketing brand strength. A sales professional who is a talent motivator known for leading by example, and driven by the desire to add value and achieve new benchmarks. Whatever the goal, I work every day to achieve it.

Tell a "story" about your job accomplishments, and do not neglect to play back the buzzwords used in the job description (if you are applying for a specific job listing).

In the experience section of your résumé, use specific examples to bring your "story" to life. If you are applying online, realize that employers will likely be using software to sort résumés to fit the job specs. So if the job requires "strong project management skills," make sure you play back these words. Here are some examples:

- Instrumental in start-up's rise to become the biotech leader in X. To create market demand, convinced company's management team to create a variation of an existing product that we sold to companies wishing to gain X experience.

- Leader with strong project management skills who repositioned non-competitive product line and developed $20 million + revenue stream by focusing on a new niche market.

- Challenged to fuel growth despite fading product set, poor internal morale and declining revenue. Refocused business areas resonated with clients, the media, consultants and employees, and led to exceeding $50 million budget goal.

Use a celebrity endorsement: As the saying goes, the best advertising is word-of-mouth endorsements from satisfied customers. And the ultimate endorsement is the celebrity endorsement. For your résumé, we are not talking about getting a testimonial from an actual celebrity. But, rather, ask a former boss, senior executive, client, or colleague if he would provide a quote about you and your abilities, or about a project you worked on.

You can place the senior executive's endorsement statement right after the profile statement at the beginning of your résumé or use it in a cover letter or as part of an Achievement Addendum at the end of your résumé that highlights in detail key achievements and accomplishments.

Here is an example of a third-party endorsement for your résumé:

CEO Martin Smith, ABC Company

"John is exceptional at team building and sales leadership, guiding team members and executives in reaching or exceeding goals. His charisma and ability to motivate a wide range of sales professionals helped the company achieve and often exceed budget goals."

Dirks: What are some common mistakes you see most people make when it comes to developing, nurturing, and marketing their personal brand?

Kaputa: 1) Not building a big network of mentors and business colleagues: Brand managers build a wide network of customers and alliances, and you should, too. The bigger your network the better, and with the Internet, it is easy to stay in touch, even if staying in touch means only one or two e-mails a year. Most people do serial networking when they are looking for a job, then let the contacts go by the wayside. And that will put you at a disadvantage to others with a wide network. You will want all kinds of people in your network, even people you know very casually—the "weak links." Every job I have gotten has come from a weak link, someone I knew casually but had kept in touch with.

2) Not developing a personal marketing plan: Brand building involves both creative work and strategic work. But the best brand ideas would go nowhere unless there is a marketing plan to achieve its goals. Likewise, you need to approach your job search like a marketing plan. Think in terms of markets targeting your key prospects. And plan specific actions as you develop a marketing plan, from A to B all the way to Z. Think creatively as you develop your marketing plan. Put attending industry conferences as part of your plan to increase your contacts, and make sure you approach people so that you have new contacts at the end.

3) Giving up too soon after too little effort: Brand managers take control of their brands. They are proactive and do not give up. Most people send in an online application and wait for a call. That is not enough. Follow up an online application with a cover letter and hard copy of your résumé. Indicate in the cover note that you applied online and this is a follow-up. You might want to include an endorsement from a former boss or colleague in the letter. I have known a number of people who have gotten interviews by sending a hard copy of the résumé to the hiring manager while others waited for a phone call or response to their online application.

Chapter 12
Maintaining a Positive Attitude & Avoiding Burnout

One of the critical keys to success in finding job opportunities is based on your ability to maintain a steady level of positive motivation. During the course of a job search, your motivation levels can bounce up and down based on what does or does not happen each day or week. The process of finding career opportunities is not easy. You can count on the trail to be bumpy and, at times, really uneven. There will be great days, good days, fair days, blah days, and days you just will not feel like getting out of bed.

A lack of motivation is one of the biggest killers of success during a job search. Look at it this way: Having to find another one is right up there as one of life's biggest stressors. The fear of the unknown ("Will I ever find another position?") and the fear of failure ("What will happen to me if I do not?") can cause all kinds of raging thoughts.

Losing motivation is a slippery slope. Once you lose it, it is hard to get it back to the levels you need to stay the course and succeed in your job search. Many people burn through money and time during their search because the bumpy road to job search success eats away at their motivation levels. Then there are those who come out strong and hard during the beginning of their search but, over a short period of time, quickly fade. Some people, facing some initial set backs in the beginning, never recover their full tank of motivation. Do not neglect your motivation levels. Job search can be like golf: most of a player's problems on the course firmly rest in his head. Great golfers can hit a bad shot but somehow manage to come back in subsequent shots. Some golfers can have a bad shot and continue to spiral until the course is pock marked with divots.

Jon Gordon on Staying Positive During A Job Search

Jon Gordon is a speaker, consultant, and author of the international bestseller The Energy Bus: 10 Rules to Fuel Your Life, Work and Team with Positive Energy and The No Complaining Rule: Positive Ways to Deal with Negativity at Work. For more information, please visit www.jongordon.com.

We are in a recession and you are out of a job. That is the bad news. The good news, says author Jon Gordon, is that by making a few key decisions you will not only make your job search a thousand times more pleasant, but you will actually make it successful.

The days following those fateful words, "We have to let you go," are dismal ones indeed. Some mornings it is tough to even get out of bed. As you scour the skimpy classifieds and job boards, grim scenarios play in your head on a repeating loop: We will lose the house…We will have to move in with my parents…I will never find work in this economy. Tangled in despair, you can barely move much less move on. Are things really as hopeless as they seem? You wonder. And if they are not, how can you clear away the dark clouds and see the light on the other side?
Jon Gordon has been where you are right now, and he has some good news: the layoff you think is bad today will actually lead to great events in the future with the right approach and action plan.

"It does not mean that you do not allow yourself to get down," says Gordon, "But rather it is all about implementing the strategies that will help you focus, make changes and turn things around."

Gordon speaks from personal experience. During the dot.com crash, he lost his own job. And that is when his journey of reinvention began.

"I thought it was the worst event of my life," recalls Gordon. "I was two months away from being bankrupt. I had a mortgage, two kids, no insurance and very little savings. I was a paycheck away from losing it all. It sounds bad. It felt bad. Seen from one point of view, I suppose it was bad. But then, one day I decided that I was not going to let this challenge take me down. And that is when I knew I had to change what I was thinking and doing.

"I saw that what I was viewing as so terrible did not have to be that way," he adds. "It was what I chose to make of it. So I made some decisions that changed everything and led me to do the work I do now as a writer, consultant, and speaker. I often joke that I went from fired to fired up. My layoff led to my life's mission and purpose. The moral of my story is that what you think is a terrible event can actually be a good thing. There is a myth that most people embark on a quest to find their destiny. But more often than not, through adversity and challenges our destiny finds us. It is during these times that we ask the important questions and make decisions that change the course of our life."

If depression, anger, and fear are your motivating factors during your layoff, you will make a tough journey even tougher for yourself and your family, says Gordon. Worse, you will hinder your own progress. Negative beliefs lead to negative actions, such as paralysis, bad choices, and shutting out friends and family. Fortunately, the opposite is also true: Positive beliefs lead to positive actions.

"We really do create our own realities," notes Gordon. "I experienced it in my own life and I have seen in the lives of others. That is why if you find yourself out of a job you must call a moratorium on negativity—anger toward your former boss, jealousy towards employed friends and ex-coworkers, worry that you will never be able to replicate your former salary—and start practicing positivity."

You may not find the positive energy switch right away, he warns. But keep looking and you will find it. He offers a few life-changing tips that can help you change your outlook and go from fired to fired up:

Jettison your anger. Allow yourself to be angry, sad, bitter, and upset for a few days, and then let it all go. Forgive the company. Forgive your employers. Release the bitterness. Know that you cannot create your future by focusing on the past. Gordon says after he was laid off, he made a conscious decision to forgive his company for letting him go and for only giving him two weeks' worth of severance pay.

"I chose to thank them, not hate them," he recalls. "Making the decision to let that bitterness go helped me to think more clearly and have more energy to take positive action. Recently I spoke with a gentleman who told me that he wished he had made the
same decision after losing his job. He said it took him a year to finally move on and that his negative energy caused him to waste a lot of valuable time."

Say to yourself, "I have a dream." Then start working to achieve it. Having studied many successful people, Gordon says he has found that they all can pinpoint the moment where they decided what they truly wanted to achieve in life. It is a practice that should be required for all of us. After all, if you know what you truly want out of life then you will do whatever it takes to make it happen. Obvious as this may sound, many people never take the time to discover it. They live on autopilot, letting circumstances shape their days, months, years, and decades.

"When I lost my job, I realized that, although I was initially sad to lose it, I hadn't been truly happy," says Gordon. "So, I took a moment and asked myself what I truly wanted to do with my life. 'What was I born to do?' I asked. 'Why am I here?' After a few days of thinking, the idea to open a franchise restaurant, which would hopefully allow me time to write, popped in my head. And off I went toward achieving my dream."

Choose to have faith in what you want, rather than what you do not want. Try out this riddle: What do fear and faith have in common? The answer: A future that has not happened yet. So why would you choose to paint that future bleak and empty, when you could paint it vibrant and fulfilling and fun?

"Fear believes in a negative future while faith believes in a positive future," says Gordon. "Even if you're not a spiritual person, why would you choose to believe the worst is going to happen? It just feels better to look to the positive future."

When you get up each morning, ask yourself this one question: What are the three things I need to do today that will help me find the job and create the success that I desire? Then, take action on those three things every day until you have achieved them. This is a great way to keep feeding your positive energy.

"You may not get there in two days, a week, or even a month," he says. "But every day you will be one step closer to your goal. And, eventually, you will get there. Or maybe you will find yourself somewhere even better."

Take on a "glass is 92 percent full" approach to the recession. Today's employment-related statistics can be hard to get out of your head when you are searching for a job. But unlike the pundits on TV who seem all too pleased to focus on the most negative numbers available, you can choose to focus on the flip side, says Gordon. Rather than fixating on 8 percent unemployment, focus on 92 percent employment.
"Dwelling on the higher number will likely be better for maintaining a positive state of mind during your job search," says Gordon. "Always remember, the choice is yours."

Choose to be humble and hungry. Be humble, advises Gordon. Know that you do not have all the answers and can learn something from everyone. Know that there are always new ways to learn, improve, and get better. Be open to advice. Be open to learning a new skill and trying a job you have not thought of before.

Also, be hungry: Seek out a mentor, take him to lunch, and model his success. Think of his life as a blueprint you can follow. Continuously improve and seek out new ideas and new strategies.

"These are two very important H-words," says Gordon. "By remaining humble and hungry after my job loss, I was able to focus on and learn the things that made it possible for me to run a restaurant, write, and speak. In short, being humble and hungry helped me achieve another great H-word: happiness!"

Of course, maybe you are not the one who has been laid off. Maybe it is your husband or wife, brother or sister, or best friend. If so, says Gordon, your job is simply to encourage and love her, says Gordon. Tell her you believe in her every chance you get. Give her strength.

"I'm a lucky guy for a lot of reasons, but one of them is that my wife did exactly this for me when I lost my job," reflects Gordon. "It made all the difference in the world. Just knowing that there is someone out there sending love and support your way can make the difficult days, weeks, and months following a layoff easier.

"Really, aren't we all in this boat?" he adds. "We all know someone who's lost his or her job. If you're wondering, what can I do for that person—well, the answer is to encourage, uplift, and support him. It will not only bolster your loved one's spirits, it will make you feel good, too. Leadership, after all, is a transfer of belief."

Here are a few tactics for making sure your motivation and attitude levels are healthy during the course of your job search:

- Stay away from negative people. Conducting your own job search campaign is tough enough; you do not need to have someone with a negative attitude bring you down with them. Find and spend time with those who are positive and are encouraging to you.

- Do not try to be perfect during your job search. Want to frustrate yourself to no end? Then become a perfectionist and drive yourself nuts. Ease up on yourself and expect that the process of finding another job will not be clean and pain free. When you stumble, pick yourself up and keep moving forward. You do not need to be a perfectionist but you do need to be relentless about staying focused on your job search campaign regardless of the setbacks.

- Do not limit yourself. You are what you believe you can be and do. Norman Vincent Peale has taught millions who have read his books about the ability to do what you put your mind to. What your mind can conceive, you can achieve. Have faith in your ability to find the job/career opportunities that will enable you to conclude your search successfully.

- Do not get in the way of yourself by letting your pride block you. Make it a point to check yourself often to make sure your pride is not the reason you miss out on opportunities to keep moving your job search campaign forward.

- You are not a victim. Fear is not your friend. Do not blame others for what you are entirely responsible for. This will lead to dead ends. There will be times when you will be rejected by one person or another who cannot help you during your search.

Gene Ladd on Pink Slip Motivation
Written by Gene Ladd and used with permission.

Gene Ladd is a writer and speaker who has published books on nutrition and phyto therapy. His forthcoming book explores the powers of thought and intention for creating one's own reality. His website is www.GeneLadd.com

There is probably no way to avoid the shock and emotional trauma of a pink slip. Imagine this: Suddenly the means for paying for all of your commitments is gone. The money you use to shelter and care for yourself, family, and loved ones is gone. The first thoughts usually are the worst possible images. No food or shelter for your family and yourself, your cars are repossessed and "nobody will like me without a paycheck."

If these feelings and images persist, you have most likely been selling yourself short. You are not a paycheck. You are a spouse, a parent, a friend, and a trusted member of the community. The important people in your life love and like you for what you are, not for what you do.

We are educated in a competitive environment and go into a goal-oriented, competitive work place. It is easy to start focusing on what we do more than what we are, but it is the simple act of being that truly defines us. If and when the pink slip comes, remember that you are the same person driving home that you were when you left in the morning. The only difference is that you have some very uncomfortable adjustments to make.

You still possess all the qualities that make you a loving spouse and parent, the same characteristics that make you a good friend, and your value to the community and your world in general is not diminished by the current loss of income. You are the same person; remember your job does not define who and what you are.

Modern science has discovered that we, for the most part, create our own realities. Our thoughts determine the scope of our lives. The last thing you need at such a time in your life and career is a low self image and a belief that the loss of a job diminishes your value.

If you are going to put your best foot forward to deal with the uncomfortable adjustments thrust upon you, an image of yourself as a loser can greatly hamper your efforts. In fact, negative images of yourself can wreck your career and bring financial hardships. It is not the actual loss of a job that can destroy you; rather, it is what you think of yourself, with or without a job.

Your thoughts will set the tone as you develop a résumé and prepare your personal marketing plan. If you believe that nobody wants you and that you are too old and tarnished, that is the very image you will present. If you see yourself as the same person, pre- or post-pink slip, this is the person you will present. You will present a good spouse, loving parent and faithful friend who is uniquely valuable to the community, the world, and a future employer.

I am sharing this with you because I want to emphasize that pink slips are not the only cause of uncomfortable adjustments. At the time I felt totally devastated having to give up my job and my career; it was a difficult adjustment. I made it more difficult by feeling sorry for myself and victimized. The ordeal helped me to develop a philosophy of life that has proven valid for me many times: _Where you are is where you are supposed to be and how you got there does not matter._

The life that came to me has been far more rewarding than broadcasting. I have become a better spouse, parent and friend. The worst things that I recall about the dark days of the adjustment are my own pessimism and self-pity. Day to day, our lives seem like a confusing briar patch on a rocky hillside. As we look back, however, the events of our lives fit together like the chapters of a fluent novel. And some of our worst episodes turn out to be blessings that helped bring us to where we are.

How many times have we dropped of a résumé and rushed home to wait for the phone call that never comes? No matter what your profession might be, right now you are a sales executive, and you are also the product. The only difference is that most sales executives need to beat the bushes and come up with a multitude of clients. You only need one.

While you need to make potential employers aware of all your skills and talents, and work history, be careful not to leave out the person. Remember, you are defined by what you are, not by what you do. There will probably be scores of résumés crossing the desk of your next employer. Some will be better than yours in terms of skills and experience, and some will not be as good as yours.

The résumé only profiles what you do or what you have done. Do not be like the doctor who thinks of patients in terms of their symptoms when there is a whole person involved. Be sure your presentation lets people know who you are, as well as what you have accomplished. It is what you are that sets you aside from the pack and determines the final match up that gets the pay-checks rolling again.

Believe that what you need is going to come to you and that the right matchup will develop for you. When you go for interviews, do not neglect the things that make you unique as a spouse, parent, friend, and member of the community. What you are, more than what you have done, will make the best impression.

Even Superman and Captain Marvel have down days once in a while. Popeye came close to losing, but always found his trusty can of spinach. We do not look up to our heroes because they were strong for every conflict. We made them our heroes and idols because they never gave up. There is nothing wrong with having a down day or a temporary meltdown, but a negative self image can destroy your health and your life.

If you continue in a state of negative emotions, you will be ill within two weeks. If you recall when you started your job, about two weeks later you were ill for a couple of days with a cold or flu. The stress of a new job typically reduces the immune level and causes the person to become ill after a couple of weeks. This is a defining time. Nobody can blame you for feeling the initial shock, but, to be the hero for yourself and your loved ones, you cannot give up.

However imperfect your job search efforts might be at this time, do not give up. Believe in yourself and your value to the world, and you will find your can of spinach where you might least expect it. It is times like this when we find out things about ourselves that we might have never discovered were it not for the uncomfortable adjustment.

Everything is constantly changing, and change develops from attractions. Change occurs because of evolvement; everything, including ourselves, is constantly becoming.

Your thoughts are the attractor of the changes in your life. If you are negative about yourself and think of yourself as a loser, the changes in your life will follow that attraction. You create your own reality. If you have the courage to put those emotions aside and hold fast to what you are, that will be the attractor of the changes in your life. We cannot avoid changes, but we can control their outcome.

One last thought: listen to your genius within. We have many intelligence centers in our body and our overall being in, addition to the brain. Listen to your heart and be open to bigger changes than you might expect. Perhaps that pink slip has set you free to follow your creativity into another field. Many people in successful businesses may have never ventured forth were it not for a pink slip at some juncture of their life.

Not everybody is a candidate for a total career change, but you should keep all of your options open. You never know, this disaster may be the blessing you have been waiting for. However you make this uncomfortable adjustment, never waiver in how you feel about yourself and your place in the world. Love yourself; the world needs you. There is an old saying in India, *"When you were born, you cried and the world rejoiced. Live your life in such a way that when you die, the world will cry and you can rejoice."*

Chapter 13
Developing Your Job Search Strategy

The foundation of any job search campaign is based on your ability to build your campaign on the basis of a concise and well-directed strategy. Understanding your marketability and the basics of developing and building your personal brand are a part of this process. This chapter is dedicated to helping you layout the basics of your strategy before you commit yourself to any kinds of job search actions.

Many people fall victim to the belief that any action taken during a job search is better than doing nothing at all. During the early phases of a job search, it is very typical for people to take a more casual approach and deploy few tactics. Many "take actions," such as e-mailing résumés to every Internet-based job site they can find and scanning the local help wanted ads and hope for the best.

As time moves on and the results remain dismal, the sense of urgency tends to ramp up. That sense of urgency to try anything and everything during a job search leads to doing things that, again, yield few results. The job search then becomes less of a campaign and more a blind hope of finding job leads and opportunities.

To avoid these job search pitfalls, you first need to flesh out the basis for your strategy so that your vision is clear and your actions going forward are purposeful as well as measurable. On the issue of measurement, you will find yourself in a better position of finding the jobs you want if you have clear and measurable goals. Developing a series of performance metrics during your job search campaign allows you to determine if any adjustments need to be made to either your strategy and/or the tactics you have chosen.

One of the many causes of anguish and frustration that eventually leads to job search burnout is the lack of a coherent and clear search strategy that is linked securely to a series of tactics (actions). Simply flooding the world with your résumé will fall well short of the mark for finding the positions that suit your career and financial and self-esteem needs. Unfortunately, the job search landscape is full of sad stories from people who mistakenly substituted job search actions for a job search strategy.

Let's review within the context of a job search the definitions of both strategy and tactics.

Strategy: the process of linking different job search approaches into a coherent plan that allows you to leverage all of the resources and tactics used when conducting your search.

Tactics: the process of how a job search is conducted is a matter of what ways you decide to use in order to implement your overall strategy.

A well thought out, concise and clearly-stated job search strategy can:

- Increase your efficiencies during the search campaign by deploying only those tactics that can have a direct impact on your job search results. You focus on implementing job search tactics that are in line with your strategy.

- Reduce the cycle time it takes you to find your targeted career opportunities because you take action only on those tactics that provide the largest opportunity for success. You do not waste your time on tactics that make you feel good because you are doing something but produce thin or no results.

If you have done your homework and figured out your marketability assessment, you should be prepared for the next stage of implementing your strategy. Part of having a clear and concise job search strategy is being able to understand your employer target list.

In the early stages of a job search, it is good to have some definition around both the industries and companies that can take advantage of the knowledge, skills, and value that you can provide them. This is why it is so critical to understand both *what you know* and *what you can do* for any industry and employer.

Let's take a look at what are your compelling skills and the relevant value they deliver to a potential employer.

Your Top Marketable & Compelling Skills (what you know): If you cannot articulate what your compelling skills are, then you will have an even harder time figuring what to do next. What makes you a compelling candidate? What differentiates you from your competitors? What can you do better than they can? How can you add value to a potential employer? These are the kinds of questions you need to have answered long before you worry about what your job search strategy will be.

Relevant Value (what you can achieve with what you know): Knowledge is not power, but, rather, applied knowledge is power. There are lots of "book smart" people in this world who do not seem to add much value to anything. You have to be absolutely confident and clear about specific "value-adds" that you bring to the table. Using your past accomplishments as an example, you should have three to six (or more) different examples of how you turn your knowledge into actionable skills that deliver specific results.

For example, let's say you are a software programmer. There are lots of software programmers out there who can write programs. What might differentiate you from other programmers? You might focus on your ability to write software in a dramatically shorter cycle time than the average programmer. Additionally, you would emphasize your proven ability to deliver product that has zero defects and requires less testing than most software applications. Again, it is not what you know; it is what you can do that differentiates you from the crowd.

Applicable Industries: Does your knowledge and skills sets have applicability to only a specific industry, or can you easily transfer them to other industries as well? In this section you want to make a full list of any and all industries where your knowledge and skills are readily transferable.

Key Industry Needs/Issues: You need to research and be up to date on the key issues facing each industry. That includes understanding both current and future issues facing each industry. How do the current industry challenges provide you with a way to leverage your knowledge and skills to deliver tangible results? What can you add to help solve these issues?

Applicable Companies: "Applicable companies" refers to any firms where your skills would be easily transferable. For example, if you have done programming work with a banking IT environment, your skills will probably transfer easily to other financial services firms (i.e., brokerage, mutual funds, etc.) as well as be transferable to consulting firms, among others. Cast a fairly wide net here that you can then pare down later in the process.

Key Company Needs/Issues: Delving into some research on companies should reveal what the key/critical issues are for them. What are they currently dealing with? What kinds of people are they hiring as a result of these issues? How can you apply your knowledge and skills to these key issues to help shape or deliver a positive outcome?

The Job Search Strategy Statement

Once you have a defined sense of who you want to target in your job search, you are ready to combine that with your top marketable skills and create a simple strategy statement. The job search strategy statement is important because it sets the tone for the entire search. You will use it as a guideline for what tactics you will deploy and where you will be investing most of your time during the search. Likewise, it will help you eliminate low-value targets and job search tactics that are less likely to bring results in a shorter span of time. More than likely, going after low-value industry/company targets and deploying low-value tactics in the mix is a prescription for much frustration and burn-out. Focus on less tactics but implement and execute them fully.

Your job search strategy statement should be clear and concise. When read by someone else, it should become immediately clear what you will be doing and why during your job search. If it leaves someone fuzzy about what you are about to do, then rework your strategy until your plans become clear.

Examples of a job search strategy statement for a Registered Nurse:

I will focus my job search campaign efforts and develop job leads within the following industries: hospitals, private medical practices of ten doctors or more, and home healthcare agencies. All RN-type positions, including those in nursing administration, will be considered as options.

I will leverage my top marketable skills/attributes with a particular focus on

_____.
Potential employers need to be located within a 50 mile radius of my home.

This simple strategy statement lays out the basic parameters for which all other supporting campaign tactics will be aligned with. It spells out several important items:

- Which specific employers, industries, or career fields are of interest to you
- The range of positions that you would consider
- Identifies the key marketable skills that will play a large role in the tactical campaign
- Provides some geographic parameters in the context of just how far you will travel or move for a new career opportunity

Again, the reason you want to take the time to develop a job search strategy statement is to leverage your efforts against the time and resources you have available. It is the rifled approach to job search campaigning instead of the shotgun approach. Your strategy statement allows you to remain focused on the key areas of your job search and not get distracted with sideshows that end up eating up your valuable time.

Conducting a job search is stressful no matter how good the job market. In a tough market, the pressure to generate results creates even more stress. A well-defined, concise, and clear job search strategy statement gives you some peace of mind. It should be referred to time and time again when you feel like your world is coming apart and it seems that there is too much to do and little time to do it in. You need something that will remind of what you need to do along the way to your next career position and a good strategy statement can do it.

Targeting High Potential Employers

During a job search, your most precious commodity is not your knowledge; it is your time. There is no way around the fact that a job search presents two challenges in the context of time: For starters, a job search can consume a lot of time by itself. Secondly, by its very nature, a job search is a source of pressure to produce another job in the shortest amount of time. The only way to balance these time pressures is by evaluating and targeting particular employers instead of trying to flood every employer with your résumé.

With that in mind, know that it is critical to target *high potential* employers before your begin your search. Unless you live in a very remote area with few employers, most people will have more than a few potential employers to include in the job search. The phrase "high potential" is important here. You want to target those employers who you know already have people with your expertise on staff.

Before you begin your job search, you need to be able to articulate an employer's must-have attributes for you to consider it for potential employment at all.

Taking time to research each potential employer within your geographic market (or even outside of it) is critical. Employers in the high potential category begin to emerge as you evaluate them against the things you appreciate from an employer. What is most appealing about its financial health; growth position within the industry; the work culture; how it treats its employees; and opportunities for career growth? Is the company growing or contracting? You can easily add your own attributes to this vetting process and do a side-by-side evaluation of various companies.

In the long run, even if you take a lower position, or any position just to keep the mortgage paid, eventually you will want to find another employer who can put you back on your career track. So, while you work a job to keep the bills paid, you should also spend some time on a viable job search plan to get you another career opportunity more in line with what you need and want.

You next step is to put specific companies within your career area (meaning that they hire people just like you) into three key categories once you have researched and evaluated them. High priority companies are those that are either currently sourcing for your type of expertise, are in a growth mode, or are preparing to expand their current lines of business. You may also consider placing a company in a high priority category based on the number of key contacts you have within the company. Assuming the company could hire you as a course of filling similar career jobs, already having some personal and/or business contacts at an "A" level firm is a huge competitive advantage in any job market.

During any job search, your goal is to spend as much time focusing on the A list or high priority companies as possible. Over time, you will discover other high priority companies to add to your network.

The "B" level or medium priority companies are just that. They present only limited opportunities until you are able to determine otherwise. Do not plan on spending any time on these companies unless you have first completely exhausted your A list.

Do not waste your time on the "C" or low priority companies.

Geographic Targeting

Carefully map out the geographic area you want to define as your job search campaign area. Some of the key questions to ponder here include:

- How far are you willing to travel every day for work? Twenty-five miles? Fifty miles? One hundred miles?
- What geographic areas are off-limits (meaning, you will not go there even if the company pays you double salary)?
- How mobile are you in terms of living in another area?

Whatever you decide here will determine how and where you will invest your time and resources. The more narrow and limited your geographic area, the harder and longer it will take to find an appropriate position. Open the geographic area too widely and you will spin your wheels a little more. You need to come up with a middle ground for the purposes of your job search. Consult with your spouse or partner for extra input.

Chapter 14
Implementing Your Job Search Plan

Once you have developed your job search strategy, it is time to layer in the specific tactics you will deploy during your campaign. There are many different tactics that you can use in order to develop job leads. Over time, you will discover new tactics and resources that can be used to expand your job search.

Marketing *You*

If you want to land a position that enables you to meet your financial and career goals, you need to become your own Marketing Manager. A job search is essentially a series of marketing tactics that are tied together by the common thread of a job search strategy.

There are four major components to organizing your job search strategy:

1. Defining your overall job search strategy
2. Choosing your initial set of job search tactics
3. Creating a calendar that sets the pace for your campaign
4. Defining exactly what you want to accomplish for each tactic

Here's how these four components are defined:

Your job search strategy: It is a written statement that puts some broad parameters around your time, energy, and resource goals.

Your job search tactics: All of the marketing tactics reviewed in this book. Before you begin your job search, decide what tactics are best suited to supporting your job search strategy. Determine which job search tactics you will implement as your campaign begins.

Your job search calendar: Allows you to input the what, who, and when of your search within a timeframe (in this case, a monthly calendar is used). The "what" is the specific action you take. For example, if you use an e-newsletter as a tactic, you want to specify what the topic would be for a particular month. The "who" are simply the targeted individuals and/or groups who will receive the newsletter. And the "when" is a specific launch date for when the action takes place.

Your job search metrics: You will also note that after answering the what, who, and when of your tactics, you need to provide your goal for that month. A goal set for any job search tactic could either be very broadly or narrowly defined.

Establishing Campaign Metrics

When conducting a job search campaign, many people relate success to going from a dead stop to finding the job opportunities they want in no time flat. The reality is much different. Job search success, can be defined as finding as many of the opportunities you really want and need for your career in the shortest cycle time possible. Job search success is really about incremental success.

Real success is measured in steps, and every step you successfully complete builds valuable momentum. People looking for a big homerun early in the job search process are usually very disappointed. Like baseball, success can be measured by simply showing up at bat and getting base hits rather than always trying to swing for a homerun.

There is nothing like the feeling you get when your job search campaign runs smoothly on all cylinders.

If you measure your success by creating metrics for each tactic you deploy, you will be able to determine if anything needs to be adjusted or changed in order to shore up performance.

Here is an example of a simple performance metric that can be used during a job search campaign:

Tactic: Identify recruitment firms that specialize in placing chemical engineers.
Performance metrics:

- *Catalog ten new firms each week*
- *Contact each by phone to introduce yourself before the end of each week*
- *Add each contact to my CMS*

Here is another performance metric example using LinkedIn within your job search campaign:

Research and find ten potential networking contacts that work for or are associated with one of my target companies each week.

When setting goals for your campaign tactics, keep in mind the following:

1. Remember the impact of the learning curve. As you begin your job search campaign, you will learn more through experience than anything else. The initial goals you set for each campaign tactic will be based on a "best guess" basis. When goal setting, keep an open mind and be flexible enough to make adjustments if circumstances and experience dictate it.

For example, you might find that it is easier than you expected to locate and network with key decision makers from a particular set of potential employers. Let's say you set a goal of networking with two contacts per week but you find that you have actually been averaging eight people per week instead. Adjust your goal to set a minimum of eight or maybe even ten contacts per week.

2. If you skip this step, you will only sabotage your own efforts. Goals are designed to keep you on track and allow you to measure your specific level of success based on your daily, weekly, and monthly output.

3. Be realistic in your goal setting. Do not set yourself up for failure by setting goals too high or too low. Goals that are attainable with some stretching on your part are the best.

4. Set up rewards for yourself based on your performance. If you meet your goals for the week, give yourself a little reward. Identify a specific reward before you begin each week (or month if you want to reward yourself on that basis). It does not have to be a big ticket item; just something that will give you that extra push during the week. Do not cheat and take the reward early or award it to yourself if you miss your goals. You only earn it if you meet your weekly goals.

Rick Bronder on Goal Setting

Rick Bronder has over thirty years experience in business, team development, long-range planning, coaching, management, and leadership development. He operates and owns a small but highly successful consulting practice, Possibility Plus. You can e-mail Rick at rbronder@gmail.com.

High-performing people know how to get what they want. They set goals and achieve those goals at a much higher rate than others. How do they do it? Well, there are many models for setting and achieving goals, but most of them follow a basic set of steps to identify and accomplish goals. Here are those steps:

1. Be sure your goals are really your goals. Focus on those goals that you want to achieve. Just because someone else is success at starting a new business does not mean that is the right goal for you. Many times we listen to our managers or coworkers and

focus in on doing something because they say it is a good goal. High performers know this strategy can only lead to defeat.

2. Base your goals on principles that are important to you. What are your values? What do you think makes a good person? What is important to you? These are some of the questions you might ask when determining your goals. If you feel that helping people is a virtue, then a goal around that concept would be a good fit for you. Begin your goal setting by identifying five to six key principles that you believe should guide your life. This process takes time and may need adjusting after you begin to execute your goals.

3. Set goals that you believe are possible for you. It is just as frustrating to set goals that are too easy as it to set goals that are too difficult. This is not to say that you should not stretch yourself. High performers do this by thinking about what they can do, and then adding a little bit more. Goals that are challenging are exciting, and achieving those goals is very rewarding.

4. Develop a metric to measure your progress. A goal without a metric is a wish. A metric is quantitative and date related. Having a goal to become rich is not an energizing goal. The definition of rich is relative. Try quantifying the goal; I will have a $10 million net worth in five years is a much stronger goal.

5. Document your goals. Physically writing your goals reinforces the commitment to them. High-performing people know that the more you write your goals, the stronger the commitment you have to achieving them. Some successful people actually write their goals on index cards and carry those cards around with them.

6. Share your goals with people you respect. Sharing your goals with others can be a very productive way to motivate yourself. A word of caution for the selection process: select only those people you respect and who return the respect for your goals. Beware of the "dream thieves" who will tell you that your goals are not attainable. Using others to discuss your goals is an effective

way to get goal adjustment and to even get some specific tips on how to accomplish your goal. An excellent person to share your goals with is someone who has already accomplished what you want to accomplish.

7. Develop objectives and action plans to accomplish your goals. For each one, break it down into manageable pieces complete with specific actions that must be done. Be sure the objectives also have metrics. High performers know that by breaking goals into objectives and objectives into action plans, the goal accomplishment process becomes more fluid and the success rate much higher. For each objective you set, establish a personal reward for achieving that objective.

8. Set up regular status meetings. Use your calendar to set these meetings. Allow sufficient time for you to review your progress. Hold yourself accountable for progress. High performers are more ruthless with themselves than with others. Document your status in a written report. Use a format similar to most project status meetings: What have I accomplished? What problems am I experiencing, and what am I doing to overcome them? What do I plan to accomplish before my next status meeting?

9. Re-evaluate your goals based on your progress. Your first action after your status meeting is to reward yourself for your accomplishments. Next, look at your progress relative to your metrics. If you are over achieving, then set your goal higher. If you are struggling, look at what you need to do to recover. Perhaps you need to adjust your goal. Having unrealistic or unachievable goals is de-motivating and can spiral into defeat. High performers are constantly assessing their goals. When you do that, you will get a much better sense of your capabilities and will get more attainable goals. Now is the time to re-write your goals to reinforce your commitment to achieving them.

Managing Your Time

Half the battle in waging a successful job search campaign pivots on how well you manage your time each day. Conducting a job search campaign requires a level of focus and motivation that can be somewhat challenging to find everyday. Typically, the energy and focus levels during the initial stages of your search will be high. Over time, you will find yourself having to re-energize and re-focus your efforts daily, which is a normal task.

Here are some strategies designed to help you manage your time effectively during your job search campaign:

1. Set up specific "office hours" that you will work within to conduct your campaign. A job search is a full time job or, if you are still employed, at least a part time job. Setting up a specific work schedule gives your search some basic structure. It also sets up the "mental picture" that you will need to treat your campaign like the job that it is. Set up your weekly and daily work schedule, and stick to it during your job search.

2. Have a list of objectives that you would like to accomplish within each day and goals you would like to hit during the course of the week. For example, you might want to set a goal for the week of finding ten new business networking connections. Your daily objective would be to average at least two new contacts into your contact management system each day. If you exceed your goal, hooray! Setting a baseline minimum series of goals is the only path to your eventual success in finding another career opportunity in the shortest time possible.

3. Maintain a steady work pace. The early temptation during a job search is to front load it by working at breakneck speed and working at that pace day and night. That is a good prescription for two things you want to avoid at all costs: burnout and motivation loss. It is enough of a battle to face a job loss or the need to change career opportunities in a short period of time. Burnout and motivation loss layered on top mean only one thing: failure. The formula for conducting your job search at a healthy pace reads like this:

Weekly goals + Set work hours + Focused attention span = Healthy, steady pace

4. Your time off is your time off. Just like you would with any other job, give yourself some time off to relax and rebalance. That does not mean you cannot take advantage of a networking opportunity or other event that is scheduled during your days off. You need to work at the pace you are used to and relax at the pace you are used to as well. Everybody is different in this respect, and you have to find your own comfort zone between working hours and your days off.

5. Focus your attention span on the mission at hand. Your mission is to find a new career opportunity within the shortest span of time possible. Anything that gets in the way of that mission is suspect. Your attention span should be focused like a laser beam within the work hours you have set for yourself each day. Do not let the refrigerator, home chores, and other sideshow items get in the way of your work time. Stay focused.

6. Reward yourself when your reach your goals. Set a specific reward for yourself when you meet or exceed your daily, weekly, and monthly goals. Maybe it is a reward to treat yourself to an ice cream, or to take a few hours to go fishing at your favorite spot during your "non-work" hours.

7. Stay flexible and nimble. No matter how long you are working your job search campaign, flexibility is always key. You never know when opportunities or new information is going to pop up and require you to act on it. Do not be set on just one way to look at things. Keep your options open even if that means giving something or someone the benefit of the doubt. Being nimble is defined as "moving with ease; agile; active; rapid…quick to understand, think, devise, etc." In the context of a job search campaign, being nimble means you are quick to act on information and move with ease to take advantage of opportunities as they arise. Being both flexible and nimble is critical to your ability to find job opportunities that can ultimately lead you to a new position.

8. Have a process for evaluating your performance on a regular basis. Like any job, conducting a job search must have a performance review component. You need a way to determine as unbiased as possible what is working and what is not. Where are you falling short? Where are you meeting or exceeding your goals? What can be done to shore up areas of your job search that have less strength than others? Who can you call upon within your network of contacts who can offer some insights and advice on a performance area of concern (not attending networking functions and a corresponding lack of results in this area, for example)?

Chapter 15
Final Words

I like to think of job search in terms of the classic Aesop tale about the Tortoise and the Hare. Just as in the moral of that tale, the journey to discover job opportunities is won by those who finish the race.

Helping you find a pipeline of job opportunities in the shortest time possible has been the overall objective of this book. As you put your job search marketing campaign together, use this book as a reference tool and refer back to it as many times as you need. At the end of the day, if you continue to utilize the job search marketing strategies noted in this book and see them through consistently, then you will be successful in your search.

Now the rest is up to you. Have hope and faith in your ability to stay the course until you uncover the job opportunities that will ultimately lead to a new job or career.

You can do this and win.

Chapter 16
About David Dirks

David Dirks is a marketing expert and strategist. As a marketing executive, his successful 18 year career includes working with everything from start-up companies to several Fortune 100 companies. During that time, he has personally faced job search challenges as a result of corporate restructurings.

In every case, David was able to successfully find new job opportunities using the same strategies and tactics noted in his book. Through his own personal experience, he has learned to apply his marketing knowledge and insights to the process of finding job opportunities that others miss.

"It's the application of my marketing experience blended with job search strategies and tactics I've learned along the way that have resulted in this book", says Dirks.

Job Search Marketing is also the result of over 24 months of intensive research focused on finding the best practices for job search strategy and tactics.

David is also a widely read, weekly business columnist for The Times Herald Record (www.recordonline.com) one of the largest circulation regional newspapers in New York State. He, along with co-columnist Rick Bronder, writes the 'Big Dogz on Business' column.

David publishes the quarterly *JSM Newsletter,* which he offers for free and is full of up-to-date information on job search strategies, tactics, and case studies for those wanting to keep their job search skills and knowledge on the sharper edge.

He is the Chief Content Officer for the popular and growing "Big Dogz on Business" blog, www.growingmybusiness.wordpress.com.

David has a *SUNY* undergraduate degree in Business Administration. He is also a graduate of both the *Global Marketing Program at Thunder-bird* and the *Strategic Marketing Program at the University of Michigan Business School.*

David is also a freelance outdoor writer, having written several books on outdoor topics and he also writes a highly popular weekly outdoor column.

For more information, visit www.jobsearchmarketing.net

Chapter 17
About
JobSearchMarketing.Net

Check out www.JobSearchMarketing.net, the online center for this book. In it you will find up-to-date information on our job search marketing workshops and seminars as well as free articles on a variety of job search topics.

You can also read the latest blog postings and participate in discussions on job search strategy. In addition, David provides a regular menu of podcasts as well as vodcasts designed to help you uncover job opportunities that others can't.

Also offered on the Web site is a free subscription to the quarterly *JSM Review*, which is an information-packed newsletter with the latest information available on the world of job search marketing. When you subscribe, each quarterly issue is conveniently delivered to your e-mail box via a printable PDF file that you can view or print.

Check back on the site often as it is constantly updated with new material, special offers, and discounts on job search marketing products.

www.JobSearchMarketing.net

Chapter 18
Become a Job Search Warrior

Take our Job Search Warrior training and find your next job in the shortest amount of time possible.

If you are in transition or already in the job market, you already know how challenging it can be to find another position. In any of our course programs, you will learn marketing skills, strategies, and tactics that will help you effectively wage an all-out war in the search for the right job for you.

All workshops and webinar's are based on the strategies & tactics outlined in the book, *Job Search Marketing*.

What makes our job search programs different from ordinary job search courses?

1. These are rigorous programs that challenge you to learn new skills and use them to maximum effectiveness. We take a "hands-on" approach to everything we do in this course, so be prepared to work and work hard. <u>This could be one of the most important investments you will make in both yourself and your future.</u>

2. We focus on the real-world challenges of career transition or new job search. There is no fluff here. There are plenty of run-of-the-mill job search courses out there that cost less and deliver even less.

3. Our job search courses are designed to teach you job search skills that most job seekers never consider in the course of finding a new job or transitioning to another career. We intensely focus on the skills that are needed in a 21st century market. These skills will serve you well beyond your next position. They are designed to help you create a strong advancement point in which to continually grow and prosper.

A Sampling of Job Search Marketing Workshops & Webinar's*:

*Subject to change at anytime. For a current listing of available programs, dates, and locations, request the latest program bulletin by emailing at:

jsmtraining@gmail.com

Job Search Marketing—The Master Course
Overview: This course takes you through the entire process of creating a cohesive and powerful job search campaign to help you find job opportunities in the shortest time possible. Based on the book, *Job Search Marketing*. This is a comprehensive program that covers the specific elements and skills needed to develop and implement a powerful and effective job search marketing campaign.

Personal Branding and Job Search
Overview: Designed to take you through specific strategies and tactics for developing and expanding your personal brand in relation to a job search campaign. Learn how to integrate both traditional and Web 2.0+ personal branding resources and techniques to leverage your ability to generate job opportunities during your job search campaign.

Developing Your Job Search Strategy
Overview: The foundation of any job search campaign is based on your ability to build your campaign on the basis of a concise and well-directed strategy. Of the many causes of anguish and frustration that eventually leads to job search burnout is the lack of a coherent

and clear job search strategy that is linked securely to a series of tactics (actions). This course focuses specifically on the process of developing a concise and written job search strategy and how to join the specific tactics needed to carry it out to success.

The Two Faces of Networking

Overview: Business networking plays a huge role in job search marketing campaigns. Learn how to harness both traditional and Web 2.0+ platforms. This class covers specific strategies used to make the most of your time and networking efforts within the context of a job search campaign. This is an intensive look at business networking and making it a key contributor to your job search campaign.

Creating & Managing a Job Search Contact Management System

Overview: The foundation to your ability to drive your job search strategy will be built on how well you are able to build momentum via your network of contacts. You will be successful in great measure based on how well you manage your contacts. The goal during your job search is to build a networking machine that has the capacity and forward momentum to work on your behalf. This course gives you the skills you will need to produce results (more network contacts and job leads) on a consistent basis as you develop and grow you business network.

Podcasting, Blogging, & Vodcasting Your Way to Job

Overview: Get with the new media program by learning the step-by-step way to create and manage podcasts, vodcasts, and blogs as a part of your job search marketing campaign. There is no better way to showcase your expertise and skills and develop your personal brand than by crafting professional looking and sounding new media platforms. Do what most people think about but never do, and find your way to more career and opportunities along the way.

Chapter 19
Help Us Update This Book

No book on a subject that is constantly undergoing some sort of change can be left unchanged for too long. This book will be updated with a revised edition and we need your help. Let us know if could improve, update, or add to any of the chapters within this book. We always strive to be as accurate and as up-to-date as possible, so any feedback you have will always be appreciated. **Make a copy of this page and send it in to us.**

Copy and fill in this form using the space below.

Mail a copy of this page to:
David Dirks
PO Box 87
Westtown, New York 10998

Chapter 20

Resources for the Job Search Campaign

For the most part, this resource section is not intended to be an exhaustive list of resources but rather, just a few that should help you on your way to planning and implementing your job search marketing campaign and beyond. You will find more resources for job search than one person could probably read and or use in a lifetime.

Web Resources:

www.linkedin.com
www.facebook.com
www.indeed.com
www.simplyhired.com
www.careerbuilder.com
www.monster.com
www.realmatch.com
www.hotjobs.com
www.craigslist.com

Book Recommendations:

Me 2.0 by Dan Schawbel (Kaplan)
Schawbel has brought branding to the next level with this book. It covers all aspects of personal branding in detail with excellent examples.

U R a BRAND by Catherine Kaputa (Davies-Black)

Kaputa has developed one of the few books on personal branding that I can recommend, and I have read a lot of these types of books.

Note: The combination of both the Schawbel and Kaputa books provides all you will ever need to build a personal brand that can withstand the test of time. Get both books if you are serious about personal branding.

Get Slightly Famous by Steven Van Yoder (Bay Tree)

Van Yoder's book was written to help those in business differentiate themselves from their competitors by "becoming a celebrity in you field and attract more business with less effort," as the subtitle says. Van Yoder gives specific strategies and tactics that can also apply to personal branding within the job search context. It is highly recommended by me and is a very good read.

What Color is Your Parachute? by Richard N. Bolles (Ten Speed Press)

If you are not sure what you want to do with your life in a career framework, then I highly recommend the latest version of Richard N. Bolles' book, *What Color is Your Parachute?*, which caters to people who are discovering or rediscovering their talents and career desires. Bolles' book has been a leader in helping people do just that and more.

Little Black Book of Connections by Jeffrey Gitomer (Bard Press)

Gitomer has written the best little book on networking I have found, period. This is the text book on networking and relationship building.

The Social Media Bible Lon Safko & David K. Brake (Wiley)

Probably the best, most comprehensive, and up-to-date guide on anything and everything dealing with social media I've found anywhere. This is a must if you are going to integrate social media platforms like blogging, podcasting, social networks, etc. into your job search campaign strategy.

The Energy Bus by Ron Gordon (Wiley)

This book was written for those of us who are facing a job loss. Gordon has written the book in a business fable style that makes it a great read. It is a great book to help deal with the challenges that will be thrown your way along the trail to job search success.

Duct Tape Marketing by John Jantsch (Thomas Nelson)

This book is probably one of the best small business marketing books on the market today. Jantsch may have intended this book for his primary audience of small business owners, but many of the marketing tactics that can be used in a job search marketing campaign are covered in *Duct Tape Marketing* in detail. It is a great all-around marketing reference book.

Talent Is Never Enough by John C. Maxwell (Thomas Nelson)

Maxwell drives the point home in this book that having talent is not enough to propel you into life. There are plenty of people who have talent but never do anything with it. You and I do not want to be one of them. This is an excellent book on a topic that few talk about or even understand.

Résumé Handbooks:

The Résumé Handbook: How to Write Outstanding Résumés and Cover Letters for Every Situation by Arthur D Rosenberg (Adams Media)

Résumés for Dummies by Joyce Lain Kennedy (For Dummies)

The Résumé.Com Guide to Writing Unbeatable Résumés (McGraw-Hill)

Made in the USA